# Praise for *The Intelligence Revolution*

'*The Intelligence Revolution* is a complete guide for business leaders who want to truly transform their organization with AI. It provides a comprehensive framework to identify and implement a company-wide strategy to put AI into action.'

David Carmona, General Manager, Artificial Intelligence, Microsoft

'Amid the dizzying array of AI uses and developments, having a straight-forward guide to what this technology is and how businesses can use it is invaluable. *The Intelligence Revolution* is an important read for any executive who wants to thrive in the AI future.'

Gary Shapiro, President and CEO, Consumer Technology Association

'Bernard Marr has written an exceptional must-read manual on the opportunities and challenges of the AI revolution... the most significant technological opportunity for any and all businesses. Learn from one of the best, gain his insights and utilize his blueprint to prepare for the greatest revolution of our time.'

Leslie Stevens, President, Ortho-Tain, Inc

'Bernard Marr has done it again! This time with a book on AI, the most transformative business and technology trend of our times. *The Intelligence Revolution* is easy to understand and packed full of real-world examples and practical templates. A must-read for any business and technology leader.'

Bruno Aziza, Group Vice President, AI and Data Analytics Cloud, Oracle

'Bernard Marr has put business leaders in the driver's seat of the intelligence revolution with this excellent AI strategy guidebook, which dives into the broad spectrum of AI capabilities and technologies. The book avoids AI hype and instead offers an intelligent alternative, a wealth of forward-looking practical advice, while consistently demonstrating how AI will drive business success when it blends with time-tested business principles, focused on people, culture, leadership, goals, priorities, strategy and governance. No business will be left untouched by the intelligence

D0141517

revolution, which is transforming and disrupting people, products and processes everywhere. Get this book and get your business moving in fast-forward with AI.'

Dr Kirk Borne, Principal Data Scientist and Data Science Fellow, Booz Allen Hamilton

'*The Intelligence Revolution* urges every business from tuna fishing to toothbrushes to embrace AI or risk being irrelevant. Marr provides a comprehensive strategic template for how to embrace and integrate AI to get the best out of your data and your people in the Fourth Industrial Revolution.'

Andy Rubin, Chair, Pentland Brands

'Explaining a complex concept with simplicity is the most difficult challenge for a writer. In this book, Bernard Marr succeeds in enabling any business manager to easily understand AI and how it can bring benefits to businesses. The book is very pleasant to read, and action orientated, illustrated with practical examples from across all industries. A must-read for the industry leaders of the future.'

Pascal Bornet, Head of AI, Automation and Digital Innovation, McKinsey & Company

'If you have ever been wondering about what AI means, or been confused and worried about the impact of AI, Bernard Marr will clarify it all in this book for you. Not only will you understand what AI is, you will understand how to embrace it and prepare to benefit from it, regardless of which industry you are in.'

Conny Björling, Head of Enterprise Architecture, Skanska Group

'Bernard Marr is an expert storyteller. In his latest book, *The Intelligence Revolution*, he hooks readers in from the start by revealing how the tuna fishing industry has advanced and transformed over the years – along with a few predictions of how the industry might look in the next 20 years. Every industry is on a similar transformation journey; companies of all sizes and types are adopting new technologies. This book provides the reader with examples, tools and knowledge of AI that is needed to increase business success, improve performance, address barriers associated with adopting AI technologies and build a company that is equipped for the future. I highly recommend this book to anyone who wants to

understand the impact of AI and wants to strategically prepare for the intelligence revolution and use AI to boost business success.'
Kate Strachnyi, Founder, Story by Data

'Packed with well-researched examples across business sectors, the learnings are converted into practical advice on how to implement a successful AI strategy. An accessible and comprehensive read for all business leaders.'
Nina Monckton, Chief Insights Officer, NHS Business Services Authority

'Bernard Marr has written an insightful book on the value of AI with tools and techniques for all companies across all industries. His simple to understand concepts demystify AI. If you needed a kick-starter to get yourself moving on your digital innovation ideas, this is the book to do it!'
Tina Rosario, Chief Data Officer, SAP

# The Intelligence Revolution

*Transforming your business with AI*

Bernard Marr

First published in Great Britain and the United States in 2020 by Kogan Page Limited

2nd Floor, 45 Gee Street
London
EC1V 3RS
United Kingdom
www.koganpage.com

122 W 27th St, 10th Floor
New York, NY 10001
USA

4737/23 Ansari Road
Daryaganj
New Delhi 110002
India

Kogan Page books are printed on paper from sustainable forests.

© Bernard Marr, 2020

**ISBNs**
Hardback    978 1 78966 437 9
Paperback   978 1 78966 434 8
Ebook       978 1 78966 435 5

---

**British Library Cataloguing-in-Publication Data**

A CIP record for this book is available from the British Library.

---

**Library of Congress Cataloging-in-Publication Data**

Names: Marr, Bernard, author.
Title: The intelligence revolution : transforming your business with AI /
    Bernard Marr.
Description: New York : Kogan Page, 2020. | Includes bibliographical
    references and index.
Identifiers: LCCN 2020005978 (print) | LCCN 2020005979 (ebook) | ISBN
    9781789664348 (paperback ; alk. paper) | ISBN 9781789664379 (hardback ;
    alk. paper) | ISBN 9781789664355 (ebook)
Subjects: LCSH: Automation–Management. | Technological
    innovations–Management. | Artificial intelligence–Industrial
    applications. | Strategic planning.
Classification: LCC HD45.2 .M37 2020 (print) | LCC HD45.2 (ebook) | DDC
    658/.0563–dc23
LC record available at https://lccn.loc.gov/2020005978
LC ebook record available at https://lccn.loc.gov/2020005979

---

Typeset by Hong Kong FIVE Workshop
Print production managed by Jellyfish
Printed and bound by CPI Group (UK) Ltd, Croydon CR0 4YY

*To my wife, Claire, our children, Sophia, James and Oliver,*
*and to everyone who will use the intelligence revolution to make*
*our world a better place*

# Contents

# About the author

Bernard Marr is an internationally bestselling author, popular keynote speaker, futurist and strategic business and technology adviser to governments and companies. He helps organizations and their management teams prepare for a new industrial revolution that is fueled by transformative technologies like artificial intelligence, big data, blockchains and the Internet of Things.

He is a regular contributor to the World Economic Forum, writes a weekly column for *Forbes* and is a major social media influencer, with his LinkedIn ranking among the top five in the world and number one in the United Kingdom. His 1.5 million followers on LinkedIn and strong presence on Facebook, Twitter, YouTube and Instagram give him a platform that allows Bernard to actively engage with millions of people every day.

He has written 17 books and hundreds of high-profile reports and articles, including the international bestsellers *Tech Trends in Practice: The 25 technologies that are driving the 4th industrial revolution, Artificial Intelligence in Practice, Big Data in Practice, The Intelligent Company* and Data Strategy.

He has worked with or advised many of the world's best-known organizations, including IBM, Microsoft, Google, Walmart, Shell, Cisco, HSBC, Toyota, Vodafone, T-Mobile, the NHS, Walgreens Boots Alliance, the Home Office, the Ministry of Defence, NATO and the United Nations, among many others.

Connect with Bernard on LinkedIn, Twitter (@bernardmarr), Facebook, Instagram and YouTube to take part in an ongoing conversation and head to www.bernardmarr.com (archived at https://perma.cc/M57W-9BJZ) for more information and hundreds of free articles, white papers and ebooks.

If you would like to talk to Bernard about any advisory work, speaking engagements or influencer services, please contact him via email at hello@bernardmarr.com.

# PART ONE

# The intelligence revolution

*Setting the scene*

# CHAPTER ONE

# The transformative impact of the intelligence revolution

Tuna fishing might seem a strange place to start a book about artificial intelligence (AI). What could commercial fishing – one of the oldest industries in the world – possibly tell us about AI and the incredible changes that are taking place in our world right now?

The answer is: everything.

For me, fishing is the perfect illustration of how the intelligence revolution will impact every business across every industry. Commonly known as the *fourth industrial revolution* (the first industrial revolution being steam/water power, the second being electricity and assembly lines, and the third being computers), the *intelligence revolution*, as I like to call it, is driven by big data and AI. And like the previous three industrial revolutions before it, the intelligence revolution is going to transform life as we know it.

We'll return to that prediction later in this chapter. But for now, I promised we'd start with tuna fishing, and that's exactly what we're going to do.

## The evolution of tuna fishing

Centuries ago, tuna fishing was a simple affair. Fishermen would set sail for an area where the tuna would typically hang out. And when they arrived, those fishermen would throw out a big net and (all being well) catch a lot of fish.

Not very scientific, was it? Except it was, in its way. Fishermen did what they did based on information – which, after all, is just a less fancy word for data – passed down from generation to generation. They would fish only in places where they knew they had the best chance of landing a big haul. They would navigate using stars and landmarks. They would assess the wind and weather, and make decisions based on what they knew.

And it worked perfectly well that way for hundreds of years. Well, most of the time. You see, celestial navigation is all well and good, but it's not so helpful on a cloudy night. Without accurate weather forecasts, storms could wreak terrible damage on boats, even resulting in loss of life. And sometimes, the fish just wouldn't be where they were supposed to be.

## Fishing gets more intelligent

Today's tuna fishing operations couldn't be more different. Boats are equipped with modern navigation tools like GPS, and they're constantly receiving accurate updates on weather conditions and even wave strength. Journeys are smoother and much, much safer as a result of all this data, and the course can be constantly tweaked to take account of changing weather conditions – or the location of fish.

Because, as fish stocks have been depleted over the years, the commercial fishing industry has had to get better at actually finding fish. Using satellite tracking, modern tuna boats know exactly where the tuna fish are. And when they catch a young tuna fish that's too small to keep, rather than immediately throwing it back overboard, fishermen can first attach a small tracker chip to its fin. Tuna spend all of their time in shoals, so if you have the ability to track just one fish, you're effectively tracking an entire shoal. Using technology like this, it's easier than ever to locate the best catch. Boats are also equipped with sonar to measure the density of fish under the surface. Only when the boat is in the best possible location, with the ideal density of fish, do the fishermen finally drop the net or lines – thereby ensuring they can catch as many fish as possible.

And back on firm land, seafood producers are also becoming more intelligent. For example, consumers of the Bumble Bee tuna brand will soon be able to tell exactly where their fish has come from, how sustainable it is, and how fresh it is, thanks to blockchain technology – which will be used to create a secure, transparent ledger detailing every aspect of the supply chain.

The fishermen of 500 years ago would barely recognize the industry as it is today. Tuna fishing has been transformed by technology – it's undergone an intelligence revolution. And the transformation has only just begun.

### The future of fishing

Fishing boats are only going to get more intelligent, with an even greater ability to track fish, monitor weather and sea conditions, navigate, and land the biggest possible catch. Couple this with modern maritime technology, including drone ships, and tuna fishing in 20 or even 10 years' time might be very different to how it is today. The fishing boats of the future may be completely automated, using robotics and AI to sail and catch fish without humans on board – meaning boats can stay out for longer, and potentially sail more treacherous waters. These unmanned drone ships aren't a figment of my imagination; Rolls-Royce is already collaborating with self-driving car pioneers Google to create autonomous ships, and the company hopes to see the first fully autonomous ship set sail later this year.

And after autonomous ships, what's next? Fish could be grown in labs and personalized to individual customers' tastes and nutritional needs. Perhaps we'll all be 3D printing tuna sashimi in our homes. It's not as far-fetched as it sounds, especially when you think that scientists are already able to grow meat in laboratories.

I can't say for sure what's in store for the fishing industry and seafood producers of the future, but one thing is certain: the industry is only going to get more intelligent.

### Introducing the intelligence revolution

So why start this chapter with tuna? It's not because I'm obsessed with tuna sashimi (although I love it). It's because, in today's hyper-intelligent, data-driven world, every industry – even the oldest industries in the world – is undergoing dramatic changes. AI is fuelling a new intelligence revolution that will transform our world. Every business, therefore, will have to find its own version of those modern tuna fishing navigation tools.

## No industry left untouched

Bottom line: your business is going to have to get smarter. This is equally true whether you're operating in one of the more obviously contemporary industries, like the tech sector, or a more traditional industry, like fishing. And it's true whether you run a global corporation or a small startup business.

Farming, for example, is undergoing a similar revolution to the fishing industry, using technology to more intelligently plan what crops to plant, where and when, in order to maximize harvests and run more efficient farms. Manufacturing is another example of a seemingly traditional industry that's becoming increasingly driven by robotics, automation, and other advances. In healthcare, big data and AI tools are helping healthcare providers monitor patients' health, predict certain conditions and provide a higher standard of care. And in retail, companies can understand and connect with their customers in a way that's completely unprecedented.

Every industry is experiencing a similar journey to the fishing industry. Innovation and change is the new norm. Those businesses that are unable to adapt to this intelligence revolution risk being left behind. Just think of the traditional fishing operation of 50 years ago competing with a fully equipped modern fishing boat, complete with sonar, GPS and the like. Which do you think would catch more fish, run a safer, more efficient operation, and prosper for years to come? I know where I'd place my money.

It's therefore time to rethink the way we all do business. For your company, this may mean rethinking the way you create products and bring them to market, rethinking your service offering, and rethinking your everyday business processes. In some cases, as we'll see in this book, it may also mean completely rethinking your entire business model.

## The unimaginable business models of the future

Many are worried that this intelligence revolution will see jobs disappear, as human workers are replaced by machines and algorithms. This is a valid concern, and it's something I'll address in more detail later in the book. But AI and the intelligence revolution will also *create* jobs and businesses – and, no doubt, whole new industries. In 10 or 15 years' time, there will be new businesses and jobs that we can't even imagine yet. In fact, a report by Dell and the Institute for the Future predicts that 85 per cent of the jobs that humans will do in 2030 don't exist yet.[1] (And if you find that prediction hard to swallow, imagine going back in time, visiting yourself in the year 2005, and explaining the concepts of a social media influencer, autonomous car engineer, or virtual reality architect!)

## Business isn't the only thing that will change

Just like the three previous industrial revolutions, this latest revolution is going to change not just the world of business, but life as we know it. Our world, and the way we live in it, is going to change forever – on a bigger scale than most people realize.

Saying that, there are those who recognize the magnitude of AI and its impact on the world. The leaders of tech giants like Google, Amazon and Microsoft are obviously among them. (As an example, Sergey Brin, co-founder of Google, has described AI as 'the most significant development in computing in my lifetime'.[2]) But if we look beyond business, we can see that today's political leaders have also emphasized the profound impact AI is having.

In the United States, a publication from Donald Trump's administration says 'We're on the verge of new technological revolutions that could improve virtually every aspect of our lives'.[3] (Under Barack Obama, the White House also issued reports on the strategic significance of AI.) Russia's President Putin has described AI as 'the future, not only for Russia, but for all humankind... Whoever becomes the leader in this sphere will become ruler of the world.'[4] Meanwhile, China currently has the most ambitious plan to become the world's AI leader by 2030.[5]

These political leaders are bang on the money. After all, AI is already intertwined in our everyday lives, and often we use it without realizing. Every time you send an email or message from your phone, the predictive text function is pre-empting what you want to say thanks to AI. In the home, Alexa is understanding your requests and responding intelligently thanks to AI. Every time you pay for something using your contactless debit card, your bank is scanning your transactions for potential fraud thanks to... you guessed it, AI.

In the future, our lives will be filled with more smart products and AI-driven services. Most of our everyday tasks and activities will involve AI in one way or another. Wearable health trackers will monitor our vital signs and identify potential conditions. (Google has even patented a toilet seat that could gauge the blood pressure of the person sitting on it.) Our homes will be able to assess and respond to our mood with soothing lighting and music after a hard day at the office. Our cars will take us from A to B with little, if any, intervention from us. Our food will be grown for us in labs and personalized to our needs. (In fact, I believe our great-grandchildren will look back and be amazed that we used to kill animals for food, just as my own children are amazed we used to live without mobile phones.)

And those are just the things we can imagine. There's plenty more coming our way that we can't yet imagine. This is the incredible power of the intelligence revolution.

## What is AI and why is it so transformative?

In Chapter 2 I'll delve into AI in a lot more detail, including how it works, what it can do, and how it's related to other technology advances. Head there for a more in-depth look at AI.

In a nutshell, AI can be described as the ability for machines to act intelligently and 'think' in ways that until recently only humans could. AI is giving machines (be they computers, robots or whatever) the power to see, hear, taste, smell, touch, talk, walk and even fly. Thanks to AI, machines can interpret the world around them, make decisions and take action based on what they've learned. As you'll see in Chapter 2, it's this ability to *learn* from data that has led to the enormous leaps in AI in recent years.

Why is AI having such a dramatic impact? Partly it's because there's so much data available in the world today. With this vast availability of data and the massive growth in computing power (which enables us to store and analyse all that data), AI has been able to advance at an incredible pace. Again, more on this coming up in Chapter 2.

But it's also because AI is not a standalone technology, developing in isolation. In each of the previous industrial revolutions, the transformation was driven by just one technology – electricity, for instance. Now, we have so many technological advances happening at once. AI is part of a perfect storm that also encompasses advances like big data, robotics, virtual reality, 3D printing, cloud computing, quantum computing, and so on. (Read more about these technologies in Chapter 2.) It's the combination of all these technologies that makes the fourth industrial revolution – the intelligence revolution – so dramatic and profound.

## About this book

Every company, from huge multinationals to small local businesses, must prepare for this intelligence revolution. This book explains how AI will impact businesses, and sets out how to prepare your business for using AI.

### Finding ways to use AI in your business

AI offers exciting new possibilities to intelligently connect with customers, create smarter products and more thoughtful services, automate and improve processes, and, ultimately, build a more successful business.

Companies of all shapes and sizes, across all sorts of industries, are already using AI to:

- better understand customers;
- predict what products or services customers want;
- understand and predict market trends;
- deliver a more personalized experience to customers;
- develop more intelligent products and services;
- automate key business processes;
- improve operational efficiency.

This book gives you the knowledge and tools you need to do the same – to turbo-charge business success, improve performance and create a more prosperous company.

### The importance of strategy

Because AI is developing so rapidly, and having such a profound impact, it can be difficult for business leaders to know where to start. How can you cut through all the hype, confusion and scare-mongering, and put AI to use in a way that's right for your business? The answer lies in developing a robust AI strategy.

After all, what's the point of investing in new technology – any new technology – if it doesn't serve your core business needs? That's what an

AI strategy is all about: identifying what you want to achieve with AI and creating a plan for achieving those goals.

With such a vast amount of data available, and mouth-watering new technologies being developed all the time, having an AI strategy ensures you don't get lost in the hype, and that you maintain a laser-like focus on your objectives.

This book walks you through the elements of a robust AI strategy in a way that any business leader can understand. It also includes innovative real-world examples from a wide range of industries – examples that I hope will both demystify AI and inspire you to see the incredible potential of the intelligence revolution.

## What to expect from this book

This book is broken down into three parts:

- This first part sets the scene for the intelligence revolution, including a look at the key technologies that enable and are linked to AI.
- In Part Two, we turn to the application of AI in business, across three main areas: more intelligent products, more intelligent services, and more intelligent business processes.
- Part Three sets out how to become a more intelligent business, by addressing the key considerations, challenges and barriers associated with adopting AI technologies.

---

**KEY TAKEAWAYS**

In this chapter we've learned:

- The first three industrial revolutions were steam, electricity and computers. Now, we're in the midst of a fourth industrial revolution – what I like to call the intelligence revolution. This revolution is driven by AI, big data and other related technologies.

- The intelligence revolution is going to transform every business in every industry, as well as our daily lives. Every business must get ready for this revolution.

- With this book, you can strategically prepare for the intelligence revolution and use AI to boost business success.

---

In the next chapter, I define AI in a little more detail and answer a critical question: how did we get to the intelligence revolution?

## Endnotes

1   Dell Technologies and Institute for the Future (nd) Realizing 2030: A Divided Vision of the Future, https://www.delltechnologies.com/content/dam/delltechnologies/assets/perspectives/2030/pdf/Realizing-2030-A-Divided-Vision-of-the-Future-Summary.pdf (archived at https://perma.cc/8668-NL4K)

2   Vincent, J (2018) Google's Sergey Brin warns of the threat from AI in today's 'technology renaissance', *The Verge*, https://www.theverge.com/2018/4/28/17295064/google-ai-threat-sergey-brin-founders-letter-technology-renaissance (archived at https://perma.cc/R8RC-UXBH)

3   The White House (2018) Artificial Intelligence for the American People, https://www.whitehouse.gov/briefings-statements/artificial-intelligence-american-people/ (archived at https://perma.cc/BM66-JYAH)

4   Russia Today (2017) 'Whoever leads in AI will rule the world': Putin to Russian children on Knowledge Day, https://www.rt.com/news/401731-ai-rule-world-putin/ (archived at https://perma.cc/AA8N-CYLV)

5   State Council of China (2017) A Next Generation Artificial Intelligence Development Plan, *gov.cn*, http://www.gov.cn/zhengce/content/2017-07/20/content_5211996.htm (archived at https://perma.cc/9V6Z-HTPV)

# CHAPTER TWO

# How we got to the intelligence revolution

As we saw in Chapter 1, the fourth industrial revolution (or the intelligence revolution) means the world is changing at an incredible pace. Ten years ago, if a director had mentioned artificial intelligence (AI) in a board meeting, chances are they would have been laughed out of the room. Now, AI plays a role in so many aspects of our lives: searching online, email spam filters, security checks for online banking, route planning for your next road trip, matching with potential dates in a dating app, Alexa, Siri... the list goes on. We're now in a position where every company needs to start thinking about AI strategically. That's quite a change in 10 years. How did we get here so fast?

In this chapter, I'll guide you through the amazing things intelligent machines are capable of today – including activities that we think of as being inherently human. (Keep in mind throughout this book that the term 'machines' can refer to computers, algorithms, robots, machinery and equipment, and even self-driving cars.)

As we delve into the capabilities of today's smart machines, you'll also get a handy primer on various AI and tech jargon that you might have heard before, but perhaps never quite got to grips with – terms like *machine learning* and *deep learning*. This isn't a tech book, however, so I'll always define these terms in plain English.

Then, we'll look at a couple of case studies that demonstrate what these modern machine capabilities mean for real life, and finish up with a whistle-stop tour through the development of AI – or, more specifically, how and why cutting-edge AI has advanced so rapidly in recent years. (Spoiler alert: it's to do with data. Lots and lots of data.)

But first, let's get a quick definition of AI and how it works.

## Defining artificial intelligence

The term *artificial intelligence* is used to describe the ability of machines to act intelligently – meaning they can act and learn independently, without being told what to do by a human. In its most basic form, AI simply means applying an *algorithm* (a problem-solving rule or calculation) to data, in order to identify patterns, make a decision on what to do next, and maybe even predict future outcomes.

At its heart, AI is about building machines that are capable of 'thinking'. It's about building machines that can interpret the world around them, learn from that information, effect change based on what they've learned, and get better and better at interpreting information over time – just as humans do.

In research and development terms, AI is split into two branches:

- *Narrow or applied AI* applies the principles of simulating human thought in order to carry out a specific task. An example of this is computers being taught to interpret patient scan images, or a banking system being able to detect fraudulent credit card transactions in real time based on previous spending patterns. Narrow or applied AI is the type we'll focus on in this book, as it's already finding many uses in business applications.
- *Generalized AI* is focused on developing intelligent machines that can turn their hands to pretty much any task, just like the human brain. This area is less advanced than applied AI and we're not yet at the point where computers can completely simulate the human brain. But, given how fast AI is progressing, we may not be far off that point.

## Nine ways machines are already more human than you might think

Even as someone who works in the field, it blows my mind to consider what's now possible with AI. Because AI is evolving at such an unprecedented rate, today's machines are capable of doing things we thought were impossible ten or even five years ago. And, crucially, they're able to carry out tasks that we often think of as being uniquely human – like reading a book or creating works of art. Prepare to be dazzled by what machines can do...

## 1. Machines can read

Facebook's DeepText tool is just one example of how machines can now read and understand text.[1] This ability is crucial for a social media platform like Facebook, where users communicate with each other largely through text. The DeepText engine is designed to help Facebook mine all that text for insights into what users are talking about – allowing the platform to deliver more content of interest and filter out spam or other content that breaches Facebook's rules. The company says its tool can understand text from thousands of posts per second, in more than 20 languages, with near-human accuracy. It can also cope with slang and idioms.

DeepText works thanks to *deep learning*, which is a cutting-edge form of *machine learning*. Both machine learning and deep learning are sub-disciplines of AI, and both essentially involve getting machines to learn in a similar way to how humans do, by interpreting the world around us, sorting and classifying information, and learning from successes and failures. Machine learning relies on *artificial neural networks* (ANNs for short), which mimic the network of neurons that makes up a human brain. When we as humans learn to walk or write, for example, the neurons in our brain learn through trial and error that sending signals to certain muscles in specifics sequences will result in us taking successful steps or writing letters. The neurons in our brain form connections that will become stronger over time as we refine our learning through experience. This is exactly how machine learning works, where we feed a computer program data so it can train its ANN. Deep learning is the leading-edge machine learning approach that uses multiple layers of ANNs (hence deep) to filter information through, just like our brain. In this way, deep learning can be applied to a wide range of tasks or problems that require 'learning'.

As well as reading and understanding text, machines can also generate summaries of the text. Microsoft, for example, has developed an AI framework that can summarize news articles.[2] This is possible thanks to *natural language processing* (NLP), which allows machines to assess a piece of text, identify the key points, and figure out what message is being communicated.

## 2. Machines can write

As if natural language processing wasn't impressive enough, we now have *natural language generation* (NLG) – which is the process of machines creating text. In other words, machines are not just able to create a summary of content, they can also *write* content from scratch without human intervention.

News organizations like the *New York Times*, *Forbes*, *Bloomberg*, and the *Washington Post* are already using AI to generate content.[3] The Press Association is using it to create 30,000 local news articles a month.[4] But machines aren't just good for creating short-form content; academic publisher Springer has released a book written by machines.[5] Admittedly it doesn't sound like the most exciting read ever (it's about lithium-ion batteries), but it certainly demonstrates the incredible things machines are now capable of.

## 3. Machines can see

Think growing cucumbers has got nothing to do with AI? Think again. One innovative young designer from Japan has put AI to use to help sort cucumbers on his family's farm.[6] Sorting cucumbers is a surprisingly complex task – they have to be classified according to size, thickness, shape, texture, colour, blemishes and so on. Using Google's TensorFlow deep learning technology, Makoto Koike has been able to automate part of this time-consuming task. First, the system takes a picture of the cucumber, and runs a quick image analysis to confirm it is in fact a picture of a cucumber. Then the TensorFlow neural network conducts a more detailed classification of the cucumber's shape and length. At the time of writing, the system can't recognize things like colour, texture or scratches (all of which would require higher-resolution pictures and more computing power), but it's certainly helping to relieve some of the burden of sorting cucumbers at the farm's busiest time of year.

This cucumber sorting process is made possible by *machine vision* (also known as *computer vision*) – another subset of AI. Machine vision allows computers to 'see', analyse visual data and then make decisions based on what they see. Think about how much visual data there is in the world today – Instagram pictures, CCTV surveillance images, infra-red sensors, and so on. This wealth of image data has meant machine vision has come on enormously, and accuracy rates for object identification have leaped from 50 per cent to 99 percent in less than a decade.[7] As such, machine vision has found a wide range of uses, including autonomous vehicles and facial recognition software. It's also being used in healthcare to assess scan images – but more on that coming up later in the chapter.

China has become a world leader in facial recognition technology.[8] A branch of KFC in Hangzhou has been testing a payment system that analyses your smile to confirm your identity and take payment (via the Alipay app), instead of paying with cash or card. And the Beijing Subway plans to use facial recognition systems to eliminate the need for tickets. In addition, police officers in Beijing wear augmented reality (AR) glasses that are able to cross-reference faces against the national database to spot criminals in real time out on the street. (*Augmented reality* is closely related to *virtual reality* (VR). But while VR creates fully immersive computer-generated worlds, AR is rooted firmly in the real world, with information and virtual objects being 'overlaid' onto real-life objects in real time. For example, with AR glasses, an engineer could look at a car engine and see explanatory images and text overlaid on top of whatever part of the engine he's looking at.)

## 4. Machines can hear

Continuing with the theme of human senses, machines can now hear as well as see. If you've got an Amazon Echo in your home, you'll know how impressive Alexa is at distinguishing sounds and recognizing voice commands (at least most of the time). Another similar example comes from the Voicea system, which is able to take minutes in meetings and create actionable recaps.

Machines can recognize a wide range of sounds, not just the human voice. One of my favourite examples is ShotSpotter's technology, which analyses the soundscape of a city and provides real-time alerts when gunfire is detected. Sensors are positioned around the city to monitor soundwaves; when a soundwave that matches the profile of gunfire is detected, the system can find the location and provide a report to law enforcement. The system is already in use in locations as diverse as Milwaukee and Puerto Rico.[9]

Neuron Soundware's technology provides another interesting example. This diagnostic tool uses machines' hearing ability to detect the early signs of failure in machinery. So in the future, if you hear a funny clunking noise while driving your car, it's entirely possible that the car itself will use AI to detect that sound, diagnose the problem and direct you to the nearest place to get it fixed... before the car actually fails. (And, you never know, your mechanic may be wearing AR glasses to help them understand and fix the problem.)

## 5. Machines can speak

If you thought Alexa's ability to speak was impressive, you ain't seen nothing yet. Google Duplex does the talking for you, so you never have to call your hairdresser or dentist ever again. Integrating with the Google Assistant digital virtual assistant, Google Duplex uses the NLP and NLG technology that I mentioned earlier in the chapter to have entirely natural conversations with humans. It can be used to make dinner reservations, schedule appointments or make enquiries for you, all over the phone. I recommend you watch a video or listen to an audio clip of it in action – it's uncanny, cleverly responding to the person on the other end of the line in a way that's so realistic they have no idea they're talking to a machine. It even replicates all the 'ums' 'ahs' and 'u-huhs' that pepper everyday human speech. At the time of writing, Google Duplex was available for use on a range of Android and iOS devices in the United States, with plans to roll it out to other countries in the near future.[10]

If this sounds vaguely familiar, remember that *chatbots* use the same NLP and NLG technology to understand questions and commands, interact with customers and answer queries in an intelligent way. These days, just about any business can put chatbots to work, and most of us can't tell whether we're interacting with a robot or a human customer service representative when we contact a company online or through a messaging app. Soon, the same will be true when we speak to companies – will we be speaking to a machine or a human? We probably won't be able to tell the difference.

Perhaps more scarily, machines can also use NLP and NLG technology to clone our voices. Chinese tech giant Baidu has revealed that its Deep Voice software can clone anyone's voice from just a 3.7-second snippet of audio, and create new speech that replicates the speaker's accent, tones and speech rhythm with incredible accuracy. To put in perspective how quickly AI is developing, in 2017 the Deep Voice tool needed 30 minutes of audio to be able to clone a voice; within just a year, that had dropped to 3.7 seconds.[11]

## 6. Machines can smell

Next time you stop and smell the roses or wrinkle your nose at an unpleasant odour, remember that machines can now detect smells just as well as humans – and sometimes even faster and more accurately.

A team at Loughborough University in the UK is developing an AI system that can analyse the chemical compounds in human breath and learn to identify potential illnesses.[12] The system uses deep learning technology to 'read' the traces left by odours in the breath, learning from the breath samples of people undergoing cancer treatment and getting better and better at identifying certain compounds in the breath. For example, the system could recognize a group of chemicals called aldehydes that are associated with stress and illness, and was able to analyse a breath sample and spot these chemicals within minutes – a task that would take a human expert hours to complete.

The Danish Marine Agency is now using a drone to patrol Danish waters on the lookout for ships that are breaking the emission laws. The drone is able to smell the exhaust fumes of passing ships to sniff out the polluters that break the laws by emitting too much sulphur.[13]

The elegant world of perfume and home fragrances is also getting an AI-driven makeover. Working with fragrance producer Symrise, IBM has created an AI system called Philyra that can learn about perfume formulas, sift through historical success data and analyse market trends across the perfume industry to identify patterns and suggest interesting new scent combinations. Symrise will be launching two AI-designed perfumes this year.[14]

## 7. Machines can move

Robotics has come such a long way in recent years. Take a look at the robots created by robotics specialists Boston Dynamics and it's clear that robots can now mimic human movements like running, jumping, navigating around objects, and picking objects up better than ever before. Chances are you've already have seen videos of their impressive humanoid robots or their famous dog-like robot, Spot.

The advances in robotic movement have been due to *reinforcement learning*, where successful behaviour or action is reinforced by a positive reward.

Similar to toddlers learning how to walk, who adjust actions based on the outcomes they experience such as taking a smaller step if the previous broad step made them fall, machines and software agents use reinforcement learning algorithms to determine the ideal behaviour based upon feedback from the environment. Reinforcement learning is another type of machine learning.

Depending on the complexity of the problem, reinforcement learning algorithms can keep adapting to the environment over time if necessary in order to maximize the reward in the long term. So, similar to the teetering toddler, a robot who is learning to walk with reinforcement learning will try different ways to achieve the objective, get feedback about how successful those ways are and then adjust until the aim to walk is achieved. A big step forward makes the robot fall, so it adjusts its step to make it smaller in order to see if that's the secret to staying upright. It continues its learning through different variations and ultimately is able to walk. In this example, the reward is staying upright, while the punishment is falling. Based on the feedback the robot receives for its actions, successful actions get reinforced.

I recently had the pleasure to meet Alter 3, another exciting development in robotics. Alter 3 is simply observing its environment and will change its movement accordingly. This 'lifelike' robot was unveiled at an opera performance at the New National Theatre in Tokyo (where else?), demonstrating something truly impressive – the ability to move autonomously to respond to the music and perform as part of the opera.[15] Could we be witnessing the beginnings of a new lifeform? Ten years ago that might have seemed like the far-fetched plot of a sci-fi movie, but today... who knows?

But machine movement isn't just about robots. Remember that self-driving cars and trucks are able to safely drive along thanks to AI technology. Drones too. And those cute little vacuum bots that look like a giant hockey puck? They also use AI (including machine vision) to detect and navigate around objects as they clean the floor.

### 8. Machines can create

Clearly machines can carry out many human tasks these days. But creativity is something that's uniquely human, right? Surely no machine could match a human's ability to imagine and create? Wrong, I'm afraid.

AI image generation is already happening. If you think about it, it's the next logical step from machine vision and machines' ability to interpret images – just as natural language generation was the next logical step from natural language processing. First machines learned to understand, then they learned to create.

Today, thanks to AI, machines can create realistic images and videos of everything from cats[16] (of course) to faces of people that don't exist.[17] And a piece of art that was generated by AI was auctioned by Christies New York in 2018 for $432,000. The abstract painting, called *Portrait of Edmond de Belamy*, was the first algorithm-generated painting sold by an auction house. It probably won't be the last.

If you want to have a go at creating your own AI art, check out Deep Dream Generator, which lets you upload an image and create a new image from it based on various art styles.[18] Outside the world of fine art (yes, cat pictures count as fine art in someone's book), AI is also being used to create things as diverse as perfume (see 'Machines can smell' earlier in the chapter), recipes and food flavour combinations. For example, IBM's Watson AI tool is also being used to develop new recipes and flavour combos with seasoning producer McCormick & Company.[19] The plan is for every McCormick developer to be collaborating with the AI system to create AI-generated foods and flavours by 2021.

### 9. Machines can understand emotions

Okay, so machines can create in ways we thought only the human brain was capable of. But emotions are definitely, completely, 100 per cent the domain of humans, right? Not quite. Not anymore.

*Affective computing* is a branch of AI and computing that involves creating systems that can recognize, interpret and process human emotions. And, as a team from the University of Ohio found, computers can, surprisingly, be better than humans at recognizing subtle emotions like 'happily surprised' and 'sadly disgusted'.[20] After all, computers are better at recognizing patterns than humans, and many people use the same facial movements to indicate the same emotions – a pattern that computers can easily recognize. The same technology can also be used to detect when someone is lying; I've worked with one insurance company that has experimented with using voice analytics on calls to detect when someone might be lying about an insurance claim.

In the future, affective computing may have many wide applications. For example, in eLearning, the learning platform could be able to detect when a learner is bored or confused. Health providers could potentially detect mental health issues, like depression or anxiety, more easily in patient consultations. Your phone might even be able to warn you not to make that phone call when you're angry.

If that sounds far-fetched, affective computing pioneers Affectiva are already developing practical AI tools that can read and respond to human emotion. The Affectiva Automotive AI solution monitors the emotional state of drivers with a view to improving road safety.[21] Using image and speech analysis, it can measure the driver's mood and the emotional reactions of other people in the car to understand what's going on behind the wheel. And when it detects something that could potentially be unsafe, the system takes action. If it detects that a driver is fatigued or distracted, for example, the system can trigger an alert for the driver. Or if it detects that the driver is angry, a virtual assistant could guide the driver to take a deep breath, or the music system could play a soothing playlist. The car could potentially take over if the driver is unable to drive safely.

## What all this means in practice – two case studies

Mind-boggling, isn't it, what machines are capable of these days? In this section we'll explore the implications of these capabilities in a little more detail, through two case studies designed to demonstrate how AI will impact our everyday lives.

### The future of healthcare

The intelligence revolution won't just transform what businesses do – the work of doctors, nurses and other healthcare professionals is set for an AI-driven transformation as well. Indeed, some of the most exciting advances happening in healthcare are the result of AI.

For one thing, the health industry is starting to benefit from the raft of data now being collected by wearable devices, like fitness trackers and smart watches. These wearable devices (along with other smart devices, like smart phones and smart TVs) make up the *Internet of Things* (IoT) – the rapidly growing array of smart, connected objects that we carry or wear on our person, have in our home, and use at work.

Thank to these IoT devices, gathering detailed health data has never been easier. For example, did you know that the Apple Watch already has the ability to take an ECG, recording your heartbeat and rhythm in the same way as hospital equipment?[22] It can also detect when the wearer has had a fall. With abilities like this, it's no wonder the latest Apple Watch is approved as a medical device by the Food and Drug Administration in the United States.[23] In another example, researchers are also racing to create contact lenses that can track blood glucose levels.[24] As wearable technology like this becomes more common, patients will be able to better manage their health and make more informed lifestyle choices, and healthcare professionals will be able to monitor patients' health data more closely and better manage their treatment.

Obviously, healthcare professionals do an amazing job, often in very difficult, high-pressure circumstances, and no one wants to see doctors replaced by robots. But, like all humans, doctors get tired, have the occasional off day and make mistakes. Machines never get tired or momentarily struggle to recall something they learned in medical school years ago. So if you can combine the work of human healthcare professionals with intelligent machines, you have the ability to automate or streamline the more routine, time-consuming tasks, like checking thousands of scan images. This frees up doctors and nurses to spend more of their precious time on patient care, deciding the best course of treatment, and so on.

Let's take the work of radiologists as an example. Radiologists train for years and do difficult, laborious work, interpreting scan images for signs of anomalies that may indicate disease. AI technology – particularly machine vision – can help lighten the load by trawling through patient scans for signs of anomalies (even in the very early stages of disease, which can be difficult to spot), and flagging those scans that need expert human analysis. In fact, this technology is already in use – take Infervision's image recognition technology as an example. Infervision's tool uses deep learning technology to look for signs of lung cancer in CT scans, and is already in use at locations across China.[25]

Your family doctor, or GP (General Practitioner), as they are referred to in the UK, is another example of how the work of human healthcare professionals could be augmented by AI. In the UK, the average appointment with your GP lasts just 10 minutes. In that squeezed time slot, the GP has to familiarize themselves with your notes, listen to your description of the problem, get a feel for your family history, conduct an examination, diagnose the problem and decide a way forward. Ten minutes is hardly enough time for all that. AI could help to get the most out of those 10 minutes and make brief consultations much more efficient. This doesn't mean robot doctors replacing humans – rather, AI could supplement the GP's work by sifting through the patient's medical records and family history in seconds to extract the most relevant insights.

## The AI-driven society

As part of China's drive to become world leaders in AI (a goal it's not alone in striving for), the country is rolling out something called the Chinese Social Credit score system. This is a bit like a financial credit score system – except it rates far more than your financial trustworthiness.[26]

The Chinese government has taken the idea of a financial credit score and applied it to all sorts of areas of life, to build a picture of how trustworthy (basically, how well-behaved) citizens are. The eventual goal is that every individual (and business) in the country will have a social credit score that takes into account everything from whether they pay their bills on time or donate to charity (which will boost their score), to whether they get a speeding ticket or cheat when playing online video games (which will lower their score). It's all combined as one score that fluctuates according to the individual's behaviour.

This is all possible because the Chinese government and private companies have access to enormous amounts of data on citizens, including financial data, social media activity, health records, online purchases, tax payments, and people they associate with.

The idea of creating more transparency around companies or individuals that break the law is all well and good, but the system has far-reaching implications for everyday life. Those with a higher score enjoy advantages like discounted energy bills, better visibility on dating sites, or not having to pay a deposit when renting a property. A high social credit score at one hospital allows an individual to see a doctor without having to queue up and pay. Meanwhile, those with a lower score may be restricted from booking airline tickets or signing up to online dating sites. They may also find it difficult to rent property.

If this all sounds like a *Black Mirror* episode set far in the future, consider this: the scheme is already up and running in some cities in China and is expected to be rolled out fully this year. Might we see a similar system adopted in other countries in future? Only time will tell.

## So how did we get here?

AI isn't a new thing. In fact, the idea of creating intelligent machines has been around for decades. American computer scientist John McCarthy coined the term 'artificial intelligence' in 1955, in his proposal for a summer AI workshop at Dartmouth College.[27] His bid was successful and the world's first artificial intelligence conference – the 1956 Dartmouth Conference – took place a year later, attended by a handful of eager mathematicians and computer scientists. The promise (and pitfalls) of intelligent machines has permeated literature, TV and film ever since.

### The birth of AI

The first artificial neural networks (ANNs) were developed in the 1950s to try to address a major stumbling block in AI: namely, while computers may be much better than humans at crunching complex calculations, spotting patterns or retrieving information quickly, they simply couldn't match the human brain when it came to interpreting the real world or completing tasks that aren't based on obvious rules. The way we recognize the face of an old friend, for example, someone we haven't seen for years, isn't a process that can be easily explained by rules. Speaking our complex and often arbitrary language is something we learn through experience over time, based on trial and error – meaning it isn't something that can be easily programmed as a simple algorithm.

ANNs would provide a major leap in simulating these human processes. In theory, instead of programming in a set of rules for the computer to learn from, you simply give the computer a bunch of data to learn from and let it figure out the rules and patterns for itself through trial and error – just as humans do. But it would take many decades to get to this point.

Why did it take so long to go from the germination of AI to the point where machines have the ability to learn and AI is so embedded in our everyday life? Two reasons: data and computing power.

## Today, data is everywhere

Today's deep learning AI is utterly reliant on data. As anyone who's learned a second language knows, the more exposure we have to a new language, the faster we pick it up. It's the same with machines' ability to learn – the more data they have access to, the faster they can learn, and the more accurate they become at interpreting the information. In this way, data is the fuel that drives AI.

Thanks to the increasing digitization of our world, we now have access to more data than ever before, which means AI has been able to grow much smarter, faster and more accurate in a very short space of time. Almost everything we do generates data, both in the online and offline worlds. Even going for a walk in the countryside generates data. Say you take a few pictures on your stroll, that's image data (and don't forget each photo contains metadata on where and when the picture was taken). Or if you buy lunch at the country pub on your debit card, that's transaction data, which your bank hoovers up to build a picture of your spending habits. What's more, our lives are increasingly filled with smart IoT devices that are constantly gathering and transmitting data every minute of every day – devices like smart phones, smart watches, smart TVs and smart speakers.

This proliferation of data is known as *Big Data*. And thanks to Big Data, AI has come on in leaps and bounds, particularly in the last five years or so.

## Computing power now packs much more punch

It takes a lot of computing power to capture, store and analyse Big Data. The recent massive advances in computing power – advances like *cloud computing*, which means data can be stored 'in the cloud' rather than on a device – are the second reason AI has progressed so far so quickly. Plus, as computer chips have got smaller and more powerful, AI tasks can now be performed on tiny devices, like smart phones. Data doesn't need to be uploaded to a centralized system to be processed; the device can handle the task then and there. This ability of IoT devices to analyse data is known as *edge computing.*

These advances in Big Data and computing power have also bought about other tech trends that both influence and are influenced by AI. These trends include VR and AR, *blockchains* (a super-secure way of storing data by replicating it across many computers – in the same way as the Bitcoin currency works), and *quantum computing* (an extremely cutting-edge field that's aiming to create vastly superior computers capable of solving the types of problems it would take a regular computer many years to solve). It's the combination of all these advances that makes the intelligence revolution so powerful, so transformative and so impossible to ignore.

---

### KEY TAKEAWAYS

In this chapter we've learned:

- AI is about building machines that are capable of human-like thought processes, like learning and decision making. In particular, the ability for machines to *learn* from data, and to learn through trial and error, is central to AI. The more data a machine has to learn from, the smarter it becomes.

- Thanks to AI, machines (including computers, algorithms, robots, machinery and more) can now carry out a wide range of tasks. They can read, write, see, hear, speak, smell and move.

- Machines are also capable of being creative and understanding emotion – things that we've always thought of as being inherently human abilities.

- AI isn't a new thing. The idea of building intelligent machines has been around for decades. The reason AI has advanced so rapidly in recent years is two-fold: the enormous growth in Big Data, coupled with impressive leaps in computing power, without which we wouldn't be able to process and make sense of all that data.

---

Now that you've got a handle on the basics of AI, got to grips with some of the typical jargon involved, and seen what today's machines are now capable of, we're ready to explore how AI is being applied in the world of business. Turn to Part Two to discover the three main ways companies are using AI to drive success.

# Endnotes

1  Abdulkader, A, Lakshmiratan, A and Zhang, J (2016) Introducing DeepText: Facebook's text understanding engine, *Facebook*, https://engineering.fb.com/core-data/introducing-deeptext-facebook-s-text-understanding-engine/ (archived at https://perma.cc/ZS3J-9RBZ)

2  Wiggers, K (2018) Microsoft develops flexible AI system that can summarize the news, *venturebeat.com* (archived at https://perma.cc/F8UB-C6E5), https://venturebeat.com/2018/11/06/microsoft-researchers-develop-ai-system-that-can-generate-articles-summaries/ (archived at https://perma.cc/6HKL-UNQC)

3  Martin, N (2019) Did a robot write this? How AI is impacting journalism, *Forbes*, https://www.forbes.com/sites/nicolemartin1/2019/02/08/did-a-robot-write-this-how-ai-is-impacting-journalism/#441cc3537795 (archived at https://perma.cc/3XWN-YYUT)

4  Marr, B (nd) Press Association: Using artificial intelligence and NLG to automate local news, https://bernardmarr.com/default.asp?contentID=1273 (archived at https://perma.cc/P972-PS5N)

5  Vincent, J (2019) The first AI-generated textbook shows what robot writers are actually good at, *The Verge*, https://www.theverge.com/2019/4/10/18304558/ai-writing-academic-research-book-springer-nature-artificial-intelligence (archived at https://perma.cc/U3VE-2RPH)

6  Sato, K (2016) How a Japanese cucumber farmer is using deep learning and TensorFlow, *Google Cloud*, https://cloud.google.com/blog/products/gcp/how-a-japanese-cucumber-farmer-is-using-deep-learning-and-tensorflow (archived at https://perma.cc/E4TQ-4WSP)

7  SAS (nd) Computer vision: what it is and why it matters, https://www.sas.com/en_us/insights/analytics/computer-vision.html (archived at https://perma.cc/8E7U-VJGF)

8  Marr, B (2018) The fascinating ways facial recognition AIs are used in China, *Forbes*, https://www.forbes.com/sites/bernardmarr/2018/12/17/the-amazing-ways-facial-recognition-ais-are-used-in-china/#3700d91f5fa5 (archived at https://perma.cc/9GUK-2CRX)

9  Marr, B (2016) Shotspotter: an amazing big data use case to tackle gun crime, *Forbes*, https://www.forbes.com/sites/bernardmarr/2016/05/23/shotspotter-an-amazing-big-data-use-case-to-tackle-gun-crime/#5caccadb17b8 (archived at https://perma.cc/RR9J-7SLV)

10  Wilde, D (2019) Google Duplex rolling out to non-Pixel, iOS devices in the US, *9to5Google*, https://9to5google.com/2019/04/03/google-duplex/ (archived at https://perma.cc/W9LF-TMDT)

11  Cole, S (2018) 'Deep Voice' software can clone anyone's voice with just 3.7 seconds of audio, *Vice*, https://www.vice.com/en_us/article/3k7mgn/baidu-deep-voice-software-can-clone-anyones-voice-with-just-37-seconds-of-audio (archived at https://perma.cc/P4JM-AZ76)

12  Soltoggio, A (2018) AI is acquiring a sense of smell that can detect illnesses in human breath, *The Conversation*, https://theconversation.com/ai-is-acquiring-a-sense-of-smell-that-can-detect-illnesses-in-human-breath-97627 (archived at https://perma.cc/7HVB-AMBA)

13  Maritime Executive (2019) Sulfur-sniffing drone to patrol Danish waters, https://www.maritime-executive.com/article/sulfur-sniffing-drone-to-patrol-danish-waters (archived at https://perma.cc/Y2NF-VRY4)

14  IBM (2018) Using AI to create new fragrances, https://www.ibm.com/blogs/research/2018/10/ai-fragrances/ (archived at https://perma.cc/8GAH-5WRJ)

15  Billboard Japan (2019) New opera starring humanoid robot alter 3 in the works for Tokyo Theatre, https://www.billboard.com/articles/news/international/8503764/new-opera-humanoid-robot-alter-3-tokyo-japan (archived at https://perma.cc/G2YN-SJFC)

16  Simonini, T (2018) How AI can learn to generate pictures of cats, *freeCodeCamp*, https://www.freecodecamp.org/news/how-ai-can-learn-to-generate-pictures-of-cats-ba692cb6eae4/ (archived at https://perma.cc/27GX-NU5Q)

17  Metz, C and Collins, K (2018) How an AI 'Cat and Mouse' game generates believable fake photos, *New York Times*, https://www.nytimes.com/interactive/2018/01/02/technology/ai-generated-photos.html (archived at https://perma.cc/EQH4-4CKP)

18  Deep Dream Generator, https://deepdreamgenerator.com/ (archived at https://perma.cc/GFL3-HKGT)

19  Robitzski, D (2019) AI trained on decades of food research is making brand-new foods, *Futurism*, https://futurism.com/ai-food-research-better-recipes (archived at https://perma.cc/77HG-3UDC)

20  Koebler, J (2014) Computers can read emotions better than you can, *Vice*, https://www.vice.com/en_us/article/gvyqw3/computers-can-read-emotions-better-than-you-can (archived at https://perma.cc/AM8B-3GHD)

21  Affectiva Automative AI, https://www.affectiva.com/product/affectiva-automotive-ai/ (archived at https://perma.cc/DWB3-DDCW)

22  Apple Support (nd) Taking an ECG with the ECG app on Apple Watch Series 4, https://support.apple.com/en-us/HT208955 (archived at https://perma.cc/EZ9P-94Z8)

23  Su, J (2018) Apple Watch 4 is now an FDA Class 2 medical device, *Forbes*, https://www.forbes.com/sites/jeanbaptiste/2018/09/14/apple-watch-4-is-now-an-fda-class-2-medical-device-detects-falls-irregular-heart-rhythm/#30ff9a2d2071 (archived at https://perma.cc/TEW7-AZ69)

24  Kraft, D (2019) 12 innovations that will revolutionize the future of medicine, *National Geographic*, https://www.nationalgeographic.com/magazine/2019/01/12-innovations-technology-revolutionize-future-medicine/ (archived at https://perma.cc/NA4C-YCX8)

25  Marr, B (nd) Infervision: Using AI and deep learning to diagnose cancer, https://www.bernardmarr.com/default.asp?contentID=1269 (archived at https://perma.cc/92U7-QHKK)

26  Marr, B (2019) Chinese social credit score: utopian big data bliss or Black Mirror on steroids?, *Forbes*, https://www.forbes.com/sites/bernardmarr/2019/01/21/chinese-social-credit-score-utopian-big-data-bliss-or-black-mirror-on-steroids/#33decefd48b8 (archived at https://perma.cc/E7FN-JM4M)

27  Childs, M (2011) John McCarthy: Computer scientist known as the father of AI, *Independent*, https://www.independent.co.uk/news/obituaries/john-mccarthy-computer-scientist-known-as-the-father-of-ai-6255307.html (archived at https://perma.cc/HU3B-ADHN)

PART TWO

# Artificial intelligence in business

# CHAPTER THREE

# Artificial intelligence in business

Which of these viewpoints best matches your own?

- AI represents the beginning of an exciting new dawn for humanity, where intelligent machines help to solve the planet's biggest challenges. From fighting terrorism and curing disease to combating the effects of climate change, AI will make the world a better place.
- AI represents the beginning of the end for humanity. Super-intelligent machines bring with them the potential to destroy life as we know it, superseding human beings as the dominant lifeform on our planet.

Perhaps, like me, you sit somewhere in the middle: fascinated and awed by the incredible things that technology can achieve, while at the same time being concerned about the potential implications.

Ultimately, it doesn't matter which side of the fence you're on. Whether you're on the side of the optimists, located firmly in the 'we're doomed' camp, or balancing precariously on top of the fence trying to see both sides – the intelligence revolution is happening. We can't undo the advances that have already been made, and technology is only going in one direction – forwards, into an ever-more intelligent future. There's no going back, in other words.

For business leaders in particular, this means one thing: AI cannot be ignored. From the smallest local business to the largest global players, every company needs to come to terms with the intelligence revolution and identify how and where AI will make the biggest difference to their business. In this way, developing a robust AI strategy is about understanding what's possible and identifying the top priorities for your business – those areas where AI can deliver the most value and really turbo-charge success.

Businesses are already using AI to drive success in three main areas:

- more intelligent products;
- more intelligent services;
- more intelligent business processes.

This chapter provides an introduction to these three uses. You'll find more detail on each area across Chapter 4 (more intelligent products), Chapter 5 (more intelligent services) and Chapter 6 (more intelligent business processes).

## Which area should you look at first?

Every business is different, and your AI priorities may not resemble those of even your closest competitor. For AI to truly add value in your business, it must be aligned with your company's key strategic goals. Therefore, developing your AI strategy means confirming what it is you want to achieve most in your business, and then identifying how AI can help you get there.

### Looking at your business from the internal and external perspective

Although there are three main ways to use AI – products, services and processes – they really fall into two perspectives:

- The first perspective is **external** – developing AI-enhanced products and services means looking at your business from the perspective of your customers or the market and identifying what you need to deliver to your customers in order to succeed. Across both product- and service-based businesses, today's most successful companies are *customer value-obsessed*, which means they're all about making customers' lives easier, understanding and anticipating their customers' needs, and solving their customers' problems – all things that AI can help with. In this book, I have separated out products and services into two chapters because both offer quite different opportunities to use AI. But, ultimately, they both come down to the same thing: delighting your customers with intelligent solutions.

- The second perspective is **internal** – making business processes more intelligent means looking at your business from the inside, assessing every aspect of your operations to see how to make the business more efficient and, in turn, more successful. This will encompass everything from manufacturing to the supply chain, to your employees. (After all, today's most successful businesses aren't just customer-centric, they're also *employee-centric*, developing smarter ways to find and attract the very best talent, and keep their people happy and engaged. As you'll see in Chapter 6, HR is just one of the operational areas in which AI is proving particularly powerful.)

From both the internal and external perspectives, AI and related technologies like Big Data, the Internet of Things, edge computing and virtual reality (VR) can help you get where you want to be. Circle back to Chapter 2 for definitions of the key terms and technologies associated with AI.

### Why you should look at all three areas – products, services and processes

If you're a service-based company, you might be tempted to skip over the product-oriented sections of this book. Likewise, if your business is product-based, you might feel the urge to ignore the services aspects.

My advice is to not skip over any of the three uses when reading this book. Even if you don't make or sell any products, still give the product-focused areas a read (in this chapter and Chapter 4). Even if you're solely a product retailer, check out the content on services (here and in Chapter 5). Even if you think the operational side of things will be too advanced for your business at this stage, you should still look at the amazing ways AI is optimizing business processes (here and in Chapter 6). To get the most out of this book – indeed to get the most out of AI in your business – you'll need to consider all three areas as you work out your AI priorities.

Why? For one thing, your AI strategy may lead you from products to services, and vice versa. Think about the most successful, most talked-about companies that exist today. Apple built its reputation on making and selling iconic products like the iPad. Nowadays, you might be surprised to learn that Apple services (such as Apple Music and Apple TV) generate more revenue than iPad sales.[1] The company is transitioning from purely a product company to a service provider, with its iconic products supporting intelligent services.

On the flip side, Amazon started as a services company but now offers many products including the Kindle tablets and the Amazon Echo smart speakers that support their overall AI and business strategy.

Another example is Netflix, which began life as a service company, but it's been producing its own original content for years, based on the company's in-depth knowledge of what customers want to watch. Today, massive Netflix hits like *Stranger Things* drive more users to the service, thereby generating more user data, which gives Netflix greater insight into viewer habits, all of which feeds into creating more original content, and the happy cycle continues.

In this way, AI can throw up surprising additions to your business model – or even lead you to an entirely new business model that you never previously considered. That's why I recommend looking at AI opportunities across both products and services.

And when it comes to internal business processes, I believe all companies must investigate the potential for more intelligent operations – because, well, what business wouldn't benefit from optimized internal processes?

Bottom line: many of the most successful companies on the planet are using AI across all three areas. AI and data is engrained in the very fabric of these companies, it's part of their DNA. Facebook, for example, sells VR products through its Oculus brand, provides AI-enabled services such as Facebook and WhatsApp, and uses AI to optimize internal processes like identifying and removing offensive content.

### That's great, but we're not a tech business...

True, the examples I've given so far in this chapter are from huge tech-based businesses, but many of the world's biggest non-tech brands are doing the same sorts of thing. One of the examples I'll return to regularly throughout the rest of this chapter is the humble trainer. Yes, you read that correctly – your running shoes are about to get an AI makeover. Companies like Nike, Under Armour and Adidas are already using AI to provide smarter products, develop new services, and optimize their internal processes. More on that coming up.

To take another example, let's say you run a company that manufactures hospital scanning equipment. That's a clear-cut product business. However, thanks to AI technologies like machine vision, it's now possible for computers to analyse patient scan images and flag potential problems for further investigation, reducing the burden on human healthcare professionals. Therefore, you may introduce image analysis services alongside your products. And by making your products smarter, you may find you're producing a wealth of data on how the scanning equipment is used – which can, in turn, be used to optimize your maintenance schedules and processes. One area feeds into the other, which feeds into the other, and so on.

Any company that wants to survive and thrive must explore ways to use AI across all three areas. Sure, you may decide that optimizing your internal processes (for example, automating your manufacturing) is several years away. Your immediate priority may be to use AI to better understand your customers so that you can give them more of what they want. That's fine – the important thing is that you consider all three areas at the outset, so that you can properly prioritize what you want to achieve and develop a robust AI strategy.

To help you get started, let's get an overview of the three areas, and look briefly at how businesses are already using AI to develop more intelligent products, services and processes.

## Creating more intelligent products

The Internet of Things (IoT – see Chapter 2) means a whole host of everyday products are getting smarter. Thanks to increased computing power, and advances in sensor technology (sensors are now smaller and cheaper to incorporate into products than ever before), we have a plethora of smart devices like smart phones, smart TVs and smart watches on the market. We even have a smart diaper that come with a built-in moisture sensor that sends an alert to your phone or a vibrating bracelet when your baby's diaper needs changing. And the diaper overhaul doesn't stop there; the next iteration of smart diapers being developed by Verily Life Services (part of Google's parent company Alphabet) will be able to distinguish between, well, let's call them Code Yellow and Code Brown nappy incidents.[2]

## The benefits for consumers

You might wonder why smart nappies are necessary when generations of parents have made do with the good old fashioned 'sniff test' (or its more advanced cousin, the 'sniff and prod test'). Isn't this a case of making products smart for the sake of it? To be clear, that's not what I'm advocating in this book. AI strategy is not about incorporating AI into everything for the sake of it; as I'll reiterate throughout this book, you must use AI strategically to get the most out of it. From a product point of view (and, indeed, from a services point of view) that means working out how AI could best benefit your customers.

So what's genuinely useful about smart diapers, you might ask? Well, consider this: it's possible to detect early signs of infection from baby's urine. The data from a smart diaper can be uploaded to the cloud for analysis, and the system could provide alerts if signs of infection are present. For new parents especially, this level of information would provide welcome reassurance.

Which brings us to the key reason why so many companies are making their products smarter: it's all about making customers' lives easier, solving their problems and removing those annoying wrinkles from everyday life. Today, consumers expect smart solutions to a whole host of everyday problems, tasks and activities, whether it's changing their baby's nappy or training for a marathon.

Which brings us to another example of smart products…

## Intelligent products in action – introducing smart running shoes

Trainers are getting more intelligent. Smart running shoes by AISportage act like a fitness tracker, but provide more specialist information for runners. Embedded with a smart AI chip that monitors movement (including gait and how feet strike the ground), the shoes provide feedback that helps runners improve their form and reduce the risk of injury.[3]

Elsewhere, Runvi is creating digital insoles that gather data and (in conjunction with a smart phone app) act as an AI running coach.[4] The insoles are fitted with 30 pressure sensors and two accelerometers that collect data on your running style, and the accompanying app provides real-time analysis of your performance and running technique. In other words, you can buy insoles that 'coach' you on how to run better and avoid running injuries. Plus, by tracking data every time you run, you build up a picture of how well you're improving over time. Anyone who's ever developed a running injury and been frustrated by not being able to run for weeks or months, or anyone who's in training for a serious running challenge like a marathon will appreciate how genuinely useful this information could be.

And it's not just running shoes that are being fitted with sensors to gather data and provide feedback. The 'wearable' technology sector is booming and the world of fitness products now includes yoga leggings embedded with sensors, smart gym shirts, and headbands that help you get the most out of your meditation session.[5]

Read about lots more examples of smart products, across a wide range of industries, in Chapter 4.

## The benefits for businesses

It's clear that smart products offer customers the tantalizing promise of making their lives easier, smoother and hassle-free. But what are the benefits to businesses? Why bother making your products more intelligent in the first place?

The obvious reason is that happy customers means higher customer satisfaction, better customer retention, more positive reviews and recommendations, increased revenue, and so on. The slightly less obvious, but no less compelling reason is this: data.

### GETTING TO KNOW YOUR CUSTOMERS – IN INCREDIBLE DETAIL

By building AI capabilities into your products, you have the ability to collect masses of data on your customers' habits and preferences: how they use your product, how often they use it, when they typically use it, and more. All this data can be used to improve product design and develop new products (and, as we'll see next, services) that better meet your customers' needs.

Building a better understanding of customers may be just one of the many business benefits of AI and data – but, in my experience, it tends to be right up there as the most attractive prospect and top priority for most businesses. That's particularly true among those companies who are just starting to explore the world of AI and Big Data. The fact is, making your products smarter is a fantastic way to build a more in-depth understanding of your customers. And in today's fast-paced world, those companies who can deeply understand – and quickly respond to – their customers' needs are thriving.

### THE CUSTOMER JOURNEY NOW COMES DOWN TO MICRO-MOMENTS

The internet and our constant attachment to mobile devices have permanently altered the customer journey. Now, when we think 'I fancy booking a minibreak' or 'What shall we see at the cinema tonight?' or 'Damn, the boiler is broken', what do we do? We reach for our phone or tablet to find a quick solution. Because life is so fast-paced these days, we're constantly making quick decisions, looking stuff up on the fly, and getting split-second answers to the things we want to know. As consumers, we expect brands to respond and instantly offer us exactly what we want in the here and now.

Google calls these intense, brief 'I want to know/do/buy/go/learn' flashes *micro-moments*, and it says, 'Today's battle for hearts, minds, and dollars is won (or lost) in micro-moments – intent-driven moments of decision making and preference shaping that occur throughout the entire customer journey.'[6] According to Google, these are the moments that really matter in marketing.

So if you want to a) create products that better respond to customers' needs and b) market those products to the people who need them most, it's vital you build up as detailed a picture as possible of the micro-moments that impact your customers' preferences and decisions. Intelligent products – and the data those products gather – help you to do just that.

### ADDING NEW REVENUE STREAMS

Interestingly, for many companies, by providing smart products they're also able to move into the services field and provide add-on services that help to meet customers' needs. John Deere is a great example of this. As a manufacturer of agricultural equipment and machinery, you'd be forgiven for thinking John Deere is the epitome of a traditional product company. Not so – at least, not anymore. By making its farming equipment smart (through in-built sensors), John Deere has for years been branching out into services like smart maintenance – whereby sensors predict when machinery might be likely to fail, which informs maintenance schedules and helps to prevent machine downtime. (You can read more about John Deere in Chapter 4.) So take note: it's not just the obviously innovative tech companies like Apple who are transforming from product companies into hybrid product-and-service companies.

## Delivering more intelligent services

As we've seen, your intelligent products may lead you into the service territory. Or perhaps your business is already a service-based company. In any case, there are many exciting ways companies are beginning to incorporate AI into their services. Here I'll touch on just a couple of examples; read more about intelligent services in Chapter 5.

### The rise of servitization/subscription businesses

Servitization, one of the hottest business model trends, is fuelled by AI and data. What do I mean by servitization? Instead of selling a product or service as a one-off transaction, servitization companies operate on an *ongoing* service or subscription model. One example that I often give to illustrate the difference is Disney versus Netflix. Disney produces a film, releases it in cinemas, and maybe it makes the company a lot of money or maybe it's a big flop. Disney won't necessarily know exactly how many people have seen the movie, whether they enjoyed it, and what other films those customers enjoyed recently. Netflix, however, has a deep understanding of its customers. It knows exactly how many people have streamed a movie or series, whether they gave up half-way through to watch something else, or whether they loved it so much they went on to watch more content by the same director, actor, and so on.

Servitization businesses have access to a wealth of valuable customer data – and, as we saw in Chapter 2, data is what feeds AI. Without data, AI is nothing. In this way, today's servitization businesses are AI-powered businesses. For example, it's AI that powers Netflix's recommendation engine, suggesting similar content that customers might enjoy based on what they've watched before and what other similar customers have also watched.

### Big benefits for customers and businesses

Particularly with a servitization/subscription model – but really with any form of AI-driven service – you have the opportunity to build a more intense relationship with your customers. You can get to know your customers and their preferences and habits in a way that would previously have seemed impossible. There's no more basing decisions on assumptions or gut feelings about how customers use your products and service – rather, you gather in-depth data on how they're *really* interacting with your offering.

Armed with this knowledge, you can tweak your offering to better suit your customers' desires – just as Netflix is able to commission more of the content its customers enjoy watching.

### Intelligent services in action – getting closer to customers through apps

Let's return to the world of sports and leisure to see how companies are increasingly offering AI-enhanced services. Both Nike and Under Armour, two huge names in the sports apparel and accessories field, made their name selling great products. Now, both are investing heavily in apps – using AI to develop a better understanding of customers and deepen their relationship with their audience.

In recent years, Under Armour has made some strategic tech-focused acquisitions, including calorie-counting app MyFitnessPal. So much so that Under Armour has become the largest digital health and fitness company in the world, working towards its vision for a digital and physical future, where smart clothing provides detailed health and fitness information.[7] Let's just dwell on that for a second: a company known for producing sportswear is now the largest digital health and fitness company on earth. Through its apps, which have been downloaded by hundreds of millions of people, Under Armour has access to data such as how much people eat, how often they work out and what sort of exercise they prefer. All of this data helps the company understand customer habits and buying decisions, so that they can provide more of the things customers really want. In this way, Under Armour sees itself as the sports equivalent of the concierge in a fancy hotel, providing a highly personalized experience to users.

Likewise, Nike is also pushing into services. They have their own running app called Nike Run Club and have recently launched Nike Fit, a foot-scanning app.[8] Apparently, 60 per cent of us are wearing the wrong size shoe, and there can be huge discrepancies in sizing across brands and styles – many people are one size in one brand, but need a different size in another make or style. All of this makes buying sneakers more of a chore, and if we get the wrong size, it can cause discomfort and even injury. Nike's app is designed to solve these problems, using AI, machine vision and augmented reality to make sure every customer gets exactly the right sized shoe. Essentially, you measure your feet using the app (which scans your feet and collects several data points, including length and width), and it recommends what size you should buy. In-store, sales associates can use the same technology to determine the best-fitting shoe for the customer's individual measurements, and record what size they bought.

This will obviously make life easier for Nike customers (for one thing, as a parent, being able to accurately measure my kids' feet every few months without having to drag them into a store is very appealing); but it also gives Nike a ton of data on customer feet sizes and fit preferences. Remember I talked about those micro-moments earlier in the chapter? With this app feature, Nike has a great glimpse into customer micro-moments ('I need new running shoes' 'What size should I buy?' and so on) – just as Under Armour does with its suite of apps. And the information Nike gathers on foot size and shape could inform the design of future products.

Therefore, just as intelligent products might feed into intelligent services, intelligent services may feed back into your products.

## Making business processes more intelligent

Now that we have apps that can accurately measure several aspects of our feet, it's not impossible to imagine that, in the future, we'll have companies seamlessly manufacturing customized shoes in their autonomous factories, based on customer fit data from foot-scanning apps. In fact, as we'll see in this section, companies like Adidas are already creating highly personalized products in automated facilities.

This is possible because AI brings with it lots of opportunities for customization and optimization – in other words, the more you understand about customers, the better you can design products and services that perfectly fit their needs. And this, in turn, means you may need to overhaul some of your business processes, such as manufacturing. Or maybe, like a lot of companies, you're simply seeking greater efficiencies in a more competitive business landscape. By incorporating AI into your internal operations, you can create a more streamlined, more efficient business that's better able to meet customers' needs.

## What do we mean by intelligent business processes and operations?

In theory, AI could be worked into pretty much any aspect of a business: manufacturing, HR, marketing, sales, supply chain and logistics, customer services, quality control, IT, finance and more. From automated machinery and vehicles, to customer service chatbots and algorithms that detect customer fraud, there are AI solutions and technologies being incorporated into all sorts of business functions.

The trick is to identify which areas are the priority for your business, and where AI will add the most value. Again, it's not about bunging in AI technology for the sake of it. Rather, it's about looking at what your business wants to achieve, and determining how AI can help you get there.

## Intelligent business processes in action – automated manufacturing

Over the past couple of decades, we've seen many a business move their manufacturing overseas in a bid to reduce operating costs. Now, thanks to the intelligence revolution, and particularly advances in robotics, more companies are able to bring their manufacturing back home to Europe, the United States or wherever they're based.

Continuing with the sports theme, Adidas trialled this idea with two highly automated factories – one in Germany (where the company's headquarters are located) and the other in Atlanta, Georgia. Known as the Speedfactory, these facilities combined 3D printing, robotics and computerized knitting to create personalized running shoes that are designed for the runner's local terrain.[9] (There's that customer-centric, customer value-obsessed business model again.)

Adidas is now taking that learning and is bringing Speedfactory technologies to produce athletic footwear at two of its suppliers in Asia. Martin Shankland, member of Adidas' executive board and responsible for global operations, says:

> The Speedfactories have been instrumental in furthering our manufacturing innovation and capabilities. Through shortened development and production lead times, we've provided select customers with hyper-relevant product for moments that matter. This was our goal from the start. We are now able to couple these learnings with other advancements made with our suppliers, leveraging the totality of these technologies to be more flexible and economic while simultaneously expanding the range of products available.[10]

Automation makes a lot of sense in manufacturing. In future, we can expect to see more of this trend towards localized and customized manufacturing, across many different sectors – demonstrating how intelligent business processes are closely linked to more intelligent products.

This example also highlights the trend towards more robotics and fewer human workers in manufacturing – a trend that shows no sign of slowing down. For example, Foxconn Technology, the world's biggest assembler of Apple iPhones, has said that human workers will be in the minority at the company within a matter of years. In fact, the company has said it will replace 80 per cent of human workers within five to ten years.[11] (And while we're on the subject of iPhones and robots, in 2019 Apple was proudly showing off Daisy, a 33-foot-long, AI-driven robot that uses five arms to rip old iPhones apart. Described as an 'iPhone destroying machine' in the press, Daisy – Apple refers to the robot as 'she' – takes phones apart and picks out the particular materials that can be used again, at an impressive rate of 1.2 million phones a year.[12] In this way, robotics and AI is also helping Apple to get better at recycling and sustainability, as well as manufacturing.)

Remember, manufacturing is just one business function where AI can make a huge difference. Turn to Chapter 6 to see plenty more examples of AI-enabled business processes.

---

KEY TAKEAWAYS

In this chapter we've learned:

- Broadly speaking, companies use AI to turbo-charge their business in three main ways: creating smarter products, delivering smarter services, and making internal business processes smarter.

- In particular, smarter products and services tie in with the trend for customer-centric businesses and servitization, where companies seek to build a deep understanding of their customers and cultivate stronger connections.

- There is a certain amount of overlap between the three aspects of products, services and business processes. Creating AI-driven products may open up new service opportunities for your business. Delivering AI-enabled services may lead to new product opportunities. Changes to your product offering may open the door to smarter business processes. And so on and so on.

- For this reason, I recommend every business looks at all three aspects when developing their AI strategy. For example, even if you view your business as a traditional product company, don't overlook the service and business processes chapters in this book. You may ultimately end up discounting AI-enabled services and business processes as not relevant or beyond your current capabilities, but it's still important to consider all three areas at the outset. That way, you can build an understanding of what's really possible with AI and identify the top priorities for your business.

This chapter has provided just a brief overview of the possibilities around smarter products, services and business processes. Across the next three chapters, I'll delve into each area in much more detail, giving lots of practical, real-world examples across a range of industries. So if you're ready to dive into the exciting world of smart, AI-enabled products, let's begin.

## Endnotes

1   Gartenberg, C (2019) How Apple makes billions of dollars selling services, *The Verge*, https://www.theverge.com/2019/3/20/18273179/apple-icloud-itunes-app-store-music-services-businesses (archived at https://perma.cc/58X5-5AH5)

2   Bridge, M (2018) Google files patent for 'smart nappy', *The Times*, https://www.thetimes.co.uk/article/google-files-patent-for-smart-nappy-kjsns0f38 (archived at https://perma.cc/BC36-MT5S)

3   Smart Shoes by AISportage, https://aiage.ca/ (archived at https://perma.cc/8563-29ER)

4   Runvi smart insoles, https://www.runvi.io/ (archived at https://perma.cc/4ZBZ-MH82)

5   Hield, H (2018) Who needs smartwatches? These 7 AI wearables can boost focus, fitness and health, *Entrepreneur*, https://www.entrepreneur.com/article/316427 (archived at https://perma.cc/74NX-SFXE)

6   Ramaswamy, S (2015) How micro-moments are changing the rules, *Think With Google*, https://www.thinkwithgoogle.com/marketing-resources/micro-moments/how-micromoments-are-changing-rules/ (archived at https://perma.cc/W5FN-AVGK)

7   High, P (2017) Under Armour is now the largest digital health and fitness company on earth, *Forbes*, https://www.forbes.com/sites/peterhigh/2017/09/18/under-armour-is-now-the-largest-digital-health-and-fitness-company-on-earth/#57448fc15dfc (archived at https://perma.cc/33Z6-EUGL)

8   Witte, R (2019) With new Fit technology, Nike calls itself a tech company, *Techcrunch*, https://techcrunch.com/2019/05/09/with-new-fit-technology-nike-calls-itself-a-tech-company/ (archived at https://perma.cc/7GW7-ZJCK)

9   Ismael, A (2018) Adidas is now making city-specific running sneakers that account for differences in terrain, *Business Insider*, https://www.businessinsider.com/adidas-speedfactory-sneakers-2018-8 (archived at https://perma.cc/C498-7M5A)

10  Adidas (2019) Adidas deploys Speedfactory technology at Asian suppliers by end of 2019, https://www.adidas-group.com/en/media/news-archive/press-releases/2019/adidas-deploys-speedfactory-technology-at-asian-suppliers-by-end-2019/ (archived at https://perma.cc/B2ZH-HEND)

11  Tang, Z and Lahiri, T (2018) Here's how the plan to replace the humans who make iPhones with bots is going, *Quartz*, https://qz.com/1312079/iphone-maker-foxconn-is-churning-out-foxbots-to-replace-its-human-workers/ (archived at https://perma.cc/6ACD-PJDT)

12  Griffin, A (2019) Apple shows off robot for tearing down iPhones as it reveals new recycling programmes, *Independent*, https://www.independent.co.uk/life-style/gadgets-and-tech/news/apple-iphone-robot-daisy-recycling-green-sustainability-a8877141.html (archived at https://perma.cc/56QZ-5SHP)

# CHAPTER FOUR

# Using AI to make more intelligent products

Smart phones, smart speakers and other intelligent products all have one thing in common: they're able to gather, send and receive information (data). It's this connectivity that makes interactions between consumers and smart products more meaningful, insightful and useful. For example, a fitness tracker gathers information on how many steps you take a day or how well you sleep, and this information is transmitted to an app on your phone, where you can interrogate the data to glean useful insights on how to lead a healthier life. What's more, the information being gathered will often include data on how the user interacts with the product, opening up potential for the product to become more responsive and personalized – like the way Amazon Alexa can tell different voices apart.

This relatively new-found intelligence in everyday objects is all thanks to the Internet of Things (IoT, see Chapter 2), and the fact that computer chips and sensors are constantly getting smaller and cheaper. As we'll see in this chapter, these days it's possible to make pretty much any device a smart product, no matter how small.

## Why the rise of smart products matters to your business

There are many advantages to making your products more intelligent. For one thing, creating smart products is often the starting point for building a better understanding of your customers – how they use your product, their habits and preferences, and so on. And this data is invaluable when it comes to improving your offering and driving future success. (Circle back to Chapter 3 for more on the advantages of smart products for businesses and their customers.)

Ultimately, everything is becoming smarter – and that trend isn't going to go away. Every company that makes products needs to think about what this trend, this desire for smart anything and everything, means for their own products and business. If you don't, you risk being left behind, and quickly. As a very brief example, I recently had to call a plumber out to my home and, while he was fixing the problem, I asked him what he thought about smart home thermostats (a product I highlight later in the chapter). He didn't have a clue what I was talking about. I was astounded – smart thermostats are a huge trend in home heating and, as of 2018, more than 1.5 million homes in the UK were already using them.[1] If smart products are making their way into your industry, at the very least you have to develop some knowledge and understanding of them.

Another example that I often use is the watch industry. I love traditional timepieces – they're beautiful objects and the mechanical side of things fascinates me. But will manufacturers of traditional, luxury timepieces like Rolex and Patek Philippe survive in this age of smart watches? Many people said the same sort of thing when digital, battery-powered watches were first introduced, predicting gloomily that mechanical watches would die a death – and of course they didn't. But the rise of smart watches is very different. For one thing, these smart watches are so much more than just watches; the Apple Watch is now capable of taking an ECG and is approved by the Food and Drug Administration in the United States (see Chapter 2). This means your smart watch can now detect and alert you to heart conditions. A year ago, my family and I went through the painful experience of losing my father-in-law far too early to an unexpected heart attack following an underlying heart condition a modern smart watch could have detected. When smart watches can do so much more than tell the time, even I (someone who adores traditional, mechanical timepieces) find myself asking, 'Should I get a smart watch?' So, while I don't think the luxury watch market will dry up altogether, it's clear that consumers expect so much more from their products these days, and watches are no different. One luxury watch maker, TAG Heuer, has already moved into this space by offering a range of connected smart watches. If I was a watchmaker, the rise of smart watches would certainly give me pause for thought.

That's not to say you should quickly load your products with AI just for the sake of it. Any time you introduce new technology, it must be done in a strategic way – the chapters in Part Three of this book will help you develop an AI strategy that works for your business, whether you want to introduce more intelligent products, more intelligent services, more intelligent business processes, or all three.

In this chapter, I really want to hammer home the message that the intelligence revolution will impact every industry and almost every type of product. And that's why this chapter contains so many examples of smart products, from the objects we have in our homes, to products for transport, work, health, and more. I hope these inspire you to think about making your own products more intelligent.

## Smart products in the home

When was the last time you left the house without your smart phone? Smart phones have changed so much about how we communicate, access information and complete life's little tasks that it's difficult to image life without them. And that little invention was just the beginning. Gradually, we've been introducing more smart goods and everyday objects into our lives, like smart watches and smart speakers. As we saw in Chapter 3, now almost everything can be made smart, from the insoles in your running shoes to your baby's nappy.

This trend for smart products has particularly taken hold in our homes, where, thanks to the IoT and AI, consumer electronic goods and home appliances are rapidly becoming much more intelligent. These products can gather information on what's going on around them and respond accordingly, making our homes more efficient, more automated and more responsive to our needs – and making the whole experience of living and being in a space more interactive. Amazon Echo speakers, complete with the Alexa digital assistant, are an obvious example of such a smart home product. But there are many more examples either already on the market or in development.

Let's take a look at some of my favourite examples from the home. These demonstrate how the market has responded to our insatiable appetites for smart products, giving rise to a whole host of intelligent everyday items. If toilet seats and toothbrushes are becoming smart (and they are, as you'll see in this section), what's next? The only limit is our imaginations.

## Smart washing machines

AI in washing machines? LG is just one of the manufacturers piling into the smart washing machine market. Its TROMM washing machine adapts washing cycles in line with the weather – for example, increasing the strength of the spin cycle if the weather's not ideal for drying clothes outside. It can also communicate verbally and give tips on removing stubborn stains. Smart washing machines are also capable of regulating the amount of detergent needed according to the weight of the load and fabrics being washed, or alerting you when you need to order more washing powder.

## Intelligent refrigerators

Your next fridge could recognize what's in your fridge, automatically monitor your inventory (for example, it could tell you your cucumbers really need using up) and order more of certain items when they run out. Or, if you're at the office dreaming of dinner, but you aren't sure whether you've got, say, cream at home, you can simply check what's in your fridge via your phone – or even ask your fridge to suggest a tasty meal based on what you've got lying around. Smart wine fridges are also on the market that can tell you which wine to buy (based on what the fridge learns about your tastes), and which food to pair with your next bottle![2]

## Smart toilets

If you've got a spare $8,000, why not invest in a Kohler Numi 2.0 Intelligent Toilet, which comes with built-in Amazon Alexa? (Perfect for multi-taskers who like to check the day's weather forecast during the morning, erm, ritual.) If this sounds like AI gone mad, think again – because, in the future, a smart toilet might just save your life. One toilet seat developed by the Rochester Institute of Technology has the ability to measure users' blood pressure, blood oxygenation levels and heart rate to detect signs of congestive heart failure.[3] Similarly, Google has filed a patent for a blood pressure-monitoring toilet.[4] Meanwhile, other smart toilet projects focus on developing toilets that can adapt to the user's physical needs by adjusting the height and tilt via voice commands – allowing people with disabilities to live more independently and/or to reduce the strain on caregivers.[5]

## AI in toothbrushes

Ever since I have known my wife she's been hoping for a way in which someone or something could brush your teeth and she reminds me regularly that it is such a massive waste of valuable time. To her disappointment, AI may not be able to physically brush your teeth for you yet but it can certainly make the process more intelligent. One toothbrush, supplied by insurance company Beam, records the time and frequency of your brushing, and uses that data to calculate your dental insurance premium – so, the better you brush, the less you pay for dental insurance.[6]

## Smart home thermostats

There are many on the market these days, but Nest is the company that pioneered smart home thermostats. The Nest learning thermostat monitors how you use your home so that it can regulate your heating or cooling automatically. For example, if you get home from work at 6 pm most days, it will learn from that and start to heat or cool your home just before you get in. It also comes with activity sensors that can assess whether anyone is home or not and adjust the temperature accordingly.

## Intelligent light switches

The Orro intelligent light switch uses AI to learn how you like to use lighting in your home and respond with the right setting. It can tell when you're in the room and switch the lights on and off without you having to do anything, and it'll adjust the lighting setting based on the time of day. For example, if you like a certain setting during the early evening when you play games with your kids and then dim the lights down to watch TV, it will learn and remember that.

## Smart home security

The Netatmo smart indoor camera will send you an alert if someone breaks into your home, and send you a picture of their face with a recording. It comes with facial recognition technology, so it can learn to recognize family members, and tell you when people are home – useful if your older kids let themselves in after school or if you have elderly parents. It even has a pet detection feature, and can send you a picture and recording of what your pet is up to at home without you (I am still waiting to get surprised by my dog Millie.)

## Smart products for mobility and transport

From bicycles, cars and trucks on the roads, to drones in the sky and ships on the oceans, there are many different ways to transport people or things from A to B. When it comes to AI and transport, self-driving cars are perhaps the first example you think of, but dig a little deeper and you'll see that they're just the beginning. Whether it's via wheels, wings or waves, this whole process of movement and transport is being transformed by the intelligence revolution.

## Intelligent cars

Most of the work around AI in the automotive industry is focused around making cars more autonomous. This autonomy is graded on a scale from one to five, with features like automated parking systems being at level one and fully 'self-driving' vehicles, capable of motoring around without a driver, classed as level five.

Electric car pioneers Tesla aren't just at the cutting edge of electric vehicles – their founder and CEO Elon Musk has maybe been slightly over-optimistic when announcing that the company will have level five autonomous vehicles, capable of driving anywhere, in 2020.[7] Tesla's cars are already packed with sensors and AI capabilities, including cameras that scan the road and atmospheric sensors that monitor weather conditions. At the time of writing, Tesla's Autopilot feature (level two autonomy) allows the car to complete tasks such as matching speeds to traffic conditions, changing lanes on the motorway and parking – but, of course, the driver must be in the car and ready to take control at any moment.

Volvo is also investing heavily in autonomous vehicles and plans to reach level four autonomy by 2021.[8] Volvo is known as a world leader in safety, so it's no surprise that safety is a key part of its autonomous strategy. In one pilot project, cars were fitted with sensors to detect driving incidents and monitor road conditions – with the aim of understanding how cars and drivers react to hazardous conditions like icy roads.

Volvo is also using AI to improve driver and passenger comfort, by monitoring what in-car functions people find most useful and which features are being underused. I remember that self-parking was on the top of my feature list when I bought one of my cars, but I have probably only used it a handful of times, and each time to show someone how cool it was. Armed with better insights about actual usage of features, car companies will be able to build in more of those features that users really want and maybe provide better training to use the features they think we should use but don't.

### The AI-powered bicycle

Middle-aged and addicted to Lycra? Or maybe you just fancy making the morning commute a little easier? You might be interested in the iWEECH e-bike, which uses AI to calculate and deliver power assistance based on factors like the weather and distance to your destination.[9] Elsewhere in the world of cycling, Tome Software is using AI to help reduce bike accidents – specifically where a car hits a cyclist from the side or behind. The tool is being designed to calculate when a cyclist is in danger and provide an alert.

### Autonomous delivery robots

When you order a takeaway or some shopping online, you might be expecting a human driver to turn up on your doorstep. But companies like Dominos, Just Eat and Co-op are instead using automated delivery robots by Starship Technologies.

These cute little robots, about the size of a minifridge, are proving so popular in my home town of Milton Keynes that when I go for my evening run, I regularly encounter them trundling along. I've also used them myself to deliver Co-op groceries and dinner from our local fish and chip shop, and I have to say it's pretty cool having a robot bring you milk for your breakfast pancakes or the British classic for dinner! Starship's robots have already clocked up more than 100,000 miles and the company has a fleet of around 1,000 robots.[10] Starship says the auto-mated vehicles are great for cities, where traditional delivery trucks are costlier and less efficient to run on short-distance journeys.

### Smart, autonomous drones

Amazon has famously trialled drone delivery for parcels, but did you know that autonomous passenger drones – that's right, robot flying taxis – might be coming to a sky near you soon? Daimler-backed aviation company Volocopter has developed a two-seater air taxi, which was successfully trialled in 2017 by taking Dubai's Crown Prince on a five-minute test flight.[11] Dubai is heavily invested in making drone taxis a reality; as well as introducing flying taxis, the Dubai Autonomous Transport Strategy aims to make 25 per cent of passenger transportation in Dubai autonomous by 2030.[12]

### Autonomous ships

We hear a lot of talk about autonomous cars hitting the roads, but what about autonomous ships taking to the seas? The world's first fully auton-omous car ferry, the result of a collaboration between Rolls-Royce and Finnish ferry operator Finferries, was unveiled in 2018. The ferry, which is named Falco, navigates and operates without any intervention from a human crew thanks to AI – although it is also possible for a land-based captain to monitor the voyage and take charge (via remote control) if necessary.[13]

There's a lot more testing to be done before fully autonomous, crew-less ships become the norm, so for now it's likely that AI will be used to reduce crew numbers, help crews make better decisions and deliver effi-ciencies for shipping companies. As an example of this, existing cargo ships can be retrofitted with AI technology, such as that offered by San Francisco-based startup Shone, which can detect and predict the move-ment of other vessels on the water.

### Smart weapons

We're well used to the autopilot function on aeroplanes, but lethal weap-ons that can operate autonomously? That will raise some serious eyebrows in many areas of society. But automatic target identification and engagement systems do exist – the 'target identification' bit meaning detecting targets such as radars, tanks and air bases using sensors, and the 'engagement' bit meaning, essentially, opening fire... albeit under human supervision.[14] The US Air Force has also tested an advanced drone capable of acting as a 'wingman' for human-piloted fighter jets or as part of a 'swarm' of drones, in both cases being controlled by the human pilot in the nearby jet. Named the Valkyrie, the drone can carry a small payload of bombs, meaning it can be used to deliver extra fire-power or even to take enemy fire in place of the human-piloted fighter jet. At a cost of around $2–3 million per drone, compared to more than $100 million for the fighter jets, these drones are a relative bargain for the Air Force.[15]

## Smart products for industry and manufacturing

I'll talk a lot more about manufacturing in Chapter 6, which is all about improving your business processes with AI. For now, let's focus on indus-try- and manufacturing-focused products – because, you guessed it, they're getting smarter. Consider the following AI-enabled products that are helping to make people's working lives easier...

### Smart glasses

Google Glass – a headset in the shape of glasses capable of displaying information and allowing wearers to access the internet – is often held up as one of the biggest smart product failures. The glasses were launched to much fanfare several years ago, yet most of the world just shrugged its shoulders and thought, 'Meh, why do I need those?' It wasn't clear what problem the product solved or how it made users' lives easier. And on top of that people didn't really want to wear the glasses in public.

Rather than give up, Google went away and came up with a new version of Google Glass, called Glass Enterprise Edition 2, which is targeted at industries rather than individual consumers. As a result of this pivot, Google Glass has found a new lease of life in settings like manufacturing, healthcare and logistics. How does it work? There's a small display screen in front of the right lens that sits just above the wearer's main line of sight (so, essentially, you have to look up to check the display, and it doesn't interrupt your vision). To the person wearing the glasses, this tiny screen in fact looks like a 30-inch screen six feet away.[16] The screen can display information to remind employees of operating procedures (such as how to assemble a product), or it can be used as an 'I can see what you see' tool, allowing a supervisor to look in on what the wearer is doing. The headset can also shoot video and record audio, making it useful for inspections and quality control. Even smarter are the HoloLens glasses from Microsoft, which provide a complete mixed reality environment where you can view and interact with holographic objects that are superimposed onto your view of the real world. This is going to transform industry and manufacturing, but also many other industries from education to healthcare.

## Smart industrial machinery

Thanks to the proliferation of tiny, inexpensive sensors, it's relatively easy to introduce AI into industrial machinery (and even retrofit it into existing machinery). John Deere, a leading manufacturer of farming and industrial equipment, has been busy making its products smart for the last decade, helping its customers cut waste and drive efficiencies through smarter machinery. For example, farm equipment can now be remotely managed from a central control hub – with AI making moment-to-moment operational decisions and the farmer monitoring data points from a console in real time in his home.

Computer vision (see Chapter 2) has proven a particularly valuable asset for John Deere. The company acquired machine learning and computer vision specialists Blue River in 2017 with a view to introducing computer vision capabilities to farm machinery. Essentially, this means the machinery will be able to 'see' crops and learn to distinguish between healthy and unhealthy crops as it passes through the field. The machinery can then target specific problem areas as and when needed, rather than spraying an entire field with chemicals – potentially reducing the amount of herbicides used by as much as 80 or 90 per cent.[17]

And in another example, John Deere has introduced a system called Combine Advisor, with cameras mounted on combine harvesters to monitor video images of grains as they're being harvested. The system can analyse the quality of the grain (for example, making sure that it isn't being damaged by the machinery), and that no grain is being ejected with unwanted stalks, leaves and cobs – thereby helping farmers reduce waste.

## Intelligent manufacturing robots

For companies that make and sell robots, integrating AI capabilities and greater connectivity is a key goal. Take leading Japanese robotics company Fanuc, which specializes in industrial robots, as an example. As early as 2015, the company was acquiring a stake in an AI startup, and in 2016 it announced a collaboration with networking specialists Cisco and smart manufacturing experts Rockwell Automation, aimed at creating an industrial IoT for manufacturing.[18] Fanuc is using deep learning to help its robots train themselves by performing the same task over and over again, learning to do it better each time. For Fanuc customers, breakthroughs like this mean they'll no longer have to program every single function a robot takes in their factory – the robots will be able to learn for themselves.

## Smart elevators

Going up? Finnish elevator and escalator company KONE certainly thinks AI is on the up, and has been (forgive the pun) elevating its efforts to collect data from its 1.1 million lifts worldwide.[19] Breakdowns or faulty lifts can cause serious disruption, so, using sensors, KONE is capturing as much data as possible from its lifts and using AI and machine learning to analyse that data. This allows technicians to predict when things might go wrong and take action in advance (a process known as predictive maintenance – read more about this in Chapter 6). This can add significant value for customers with a KONE lift in their building.

## Smart surfaces

London-based startup HyperSurfaces is developing technology that can make any surface – literally *any* surface – smart. The technology uses vibration sensors and AI to transform any object, surface or material into an intelligent surface that can detect motion and carry out commands. For example, in theory, your wooden coffee table could become the controller for your TV, lighting and thermostat. Or you could lock and unlock your front door via your car door. It's hard to imagine all the ways we could potentially use such technology (just as it would have been hard to fathom social media *before* it was invented), but apparently the company has received a lot of interest from car manufacturers.[20]

## Intelligent power plant equipment

Industrial behemoth General Electric is focusing on providing its customers with smarter, self-learning power plant equipment. GE machinery throughout power plants uses sensors to gather data, which is then analysed to understand the stresses and demands at work in the power station. Using this data, power station operators can increase or decrease production in line with fluctuations in demand, or highlight previously unnoticed inefficiencies. A typical power plant can be equipped with over 10,000 sensors, and GE has the ability to capture and analyse data from all machinery in the plant – not just machines manufactured and sold by GE.[21]

## Smart products for sports and exercise

We're all familiar with smart fitness tracker bands and apps, but circle back to Chapter 3 and it's clear that AI is being added to all sorts of sports and fitness gear, including insoles and clothing. Let's look at a couple more examples of how the intelligence revolution is impacting the world of sports products.

### Wearable technology

The incredibly competitive world of sports is fast adopting AI to help teams gain a competitive edge over rivals. For example, Australian wearable technology company Catapult makes devices that measure athletes' performance and movement using sensors like GPS, heart rate monitors and accelerometers. Catapult products are used by a whole host of teams, including Australian football teams, the Australian Olympics team, the New York Knicks and the Canadian Football League. [22]

### The sensor-enhanced basketball game

Swiss electronic company TE Connectivity is hoping to transform the game of basketball using sensors. Its vibration sensors can be placed on the basketball rim or backboard to study the exact angles and trajectories of practice shots, helping players hone their shots and understand why each shot is a hit or miss. Meanwhile, altimeters can be placed in players' shoes to track speed, and accelerometers embedded in the uniform can measure jump rate, height and rotation. Even the court itself can be made smart, with TE Connectivity's sensors embedded into the surface – meaning referees can rule more accurately when a shot is out of bounds.[23]

### Smart boxing gloves

Sport sensor specialist PIQ's collaboration with Everlast is bringing the intelligence revolution to the boxing ring. The PIQ ROBOT Blue product is a smart wrist strap that analyses workouts in such detail 'it's almost unfair.'[24] It can track all the boxer's workouts, including shadow boxing and sparring, to measure factors such as punching speed, G-force at impact and retraction time. Armed with this information, the boxer knows exactly where their strengths and weaknesses lie, so that they can target their workouts on areas that need improving.

## Smart products for the health sector

In Chapter 2, I outlined how the intelligence revolution may transform the world of healthcare, from automating some of the work of under-pressure healthcare professionals, to helping individuals make better health and lifestyle choices. Many of us want to measure and monitor our own health as we go about our everyday lives – and, as a result, healthcare professionals could potentially have access to amazingly detailed and valuable data on the health of patients. Not only will this (in theory) help us all live healthier lives, many hope it will kickstart a wave of 'preventative medicine', where the onus is on stopping people getting ill in the first place, rather than treating illnesses when they occur.

This is an area I'm particularly excited about. Let's look at some of my favourite examples of smart healthcare-related products.

### Smart pee sticks

We already have smart toilets on the way, so why shouldn't we have smart urine testing sticks? After all, urine contains vital data on your diet and hormones, and is a common way to detect signs of infection. The Bisu smart urine analyser, due to hit the market this year, consists of a test stick with a biodegradable test chip. It slides out from its casing and dips an absorbent pad into the stream of urine, before sliding back in and performing a test on the urine (the test stick is then released for disposal). Going back to the smart toilet idea, my vision would be to combine the smart toilet with the intelligent pee analysis so the toilet can alert you to any potential health issues as they arise.

### Intelligent contact lenses

With Google Glass being adopted in some industries, are smart contact lenses the next step? A number of companies including Samsung, Sony and Google parent company Alphabet have been researching smart contact lens technology that could enhance our human vision or be used to monitor our health.[25] Researchers at the University of Wisconsin have been developing a contact lens that autofocuses within milliseconds.[26] Elsewhere, a team of Korean researchers have been testing a contact lens designed to monitor the blood glucose level of people with diabetes.[27]

### Smart medical imaging equipment

GE, which has said it has 500,000 medical imaging devices on the global market, has been partnering with tech company NVIDIA to integrate AI into imaging equipment to improve the speed and accuracy of CT scans.[28] Algorithms are being used to spot the small signs of organ damage that might be missed by the human eye, potentially aiding faster, earlier diagnosis of conditions. Faster scans also mean patients are exposed to less radiation.

### It's called the Internet of Medical Things

The above examples of connected medical devices and applications all essentially fall under the umbrella description of the IoMT, or Internet of Medical Things. IoMT devices can collect data, monitor activity and vital signs and notify users, caregivers or healthcare providers when intervention is needed – for example, if someone has had a fall, when a patient has forgotten to take their medication, or when there are signs of infection or illness. All of this could help to keep people safe and healthy, and lower the cost of healthcare. What's more, with the wealth of data that it's now possible to collect, healthcare providers will be able to deliver much more personalized healthcare for each individual patient.

---

**KEY TAKEAWAYS**

In this chapter we've learned:

- By their very nature, smart products produce a wealth of data that can be used for generating better customer insights and improving your offering.

- Across all facets of life – home, travel, work, health, etc – products are becoming more intelligent thanks to AI and the IoT. This is happening now, in every industry. If toilets are becoming smart, there's no limit to what can, and will, be made smart in the future.

- If you don't consider the impact of smart products on your business, and the potential to introduce AI into your products, you risk being left behind.

---

Another interesting aspect of smart products is that they often enable more intelligent services. When you produce a smart product, you may find it opens the door to potentially lucrative service opportunities, particularly subscription models; for example, some manufacturers of smart home security systems have moved into the services field, offering subscriptions to monitor your home for you, based on the data gathered by your smart security system. In this way, there's very often a great deal of crossover between smart products and smart services. Which brings us nicely to the next chapter.

## Endnotes

1 Utility Week (nd) Smart thermostats now in 1.5 million homes, https://utilityweek.co.uk/smart-thermostats-now-in-1-5-million-homes/ (archived at https://perma.cc/856V-7AA4)
2 Crist, F (2019) LG's smart wine fridge can recommend a good cheese pairing, *CNET*, https://www.cnet.com/news/lg-signature-kitchen-suite-smart-wine-column-fridge-can-recommend-a-good-cheese-pairing/ (archived at https://perma.cc/4QW6-BXDJ)
3 Med-tech Innovation (2019) The toilet seat that monitors your heart rate, https://www.med-technews.com/news/toilet-seat-that-monitors-heart-rate-and-blood-pressure-deve/ (archived at https://perma.cc/RMB3-2KTD)
4 Google Patents (nd) Noninvasive determination of cardiac health and other functional states and trends for human physiological systems, https://patents.google.com/patent/US10064582B2/en (archived at https://perma.cc/6TJJ-23EM)

5   iToilet (nd) iToilet project description and results, http://www.aat.tuwien.ac.at/itoilet/ (archived at https://perma.cc/F67D-FRWV)

6   Beam Dental, https://beam.dental/ (archived at https://perma.cc/P5LD-L4F9)

7   Hawkins, A (2019) It's Elon Musk vs everyone else in the race for fully driverless cars, *The Verge*, https://www.theverge.com/2019/4/24/18512580/elon-musk-tesla-driverless-cars-lidar-simulation-waymo (archived at https://perma.cc/NK43-HE9B)

8   Holmes, J (2018) Volvo promises self-driving 2021 XC90 you can nap in, *CNET*, https://www.cnet.com/roadshow/news/2021-volvo-xc90-autonomous-level-4/ (archived at https://perma.cc/DW9U-4A5J)

9   Mashable (2019) This ebike uses artificial intelligence, https://mashable.com/video/ebike-artificial-intelligence/?europe=true (archived at https://perma.cc/5D37-FNZ7)

10  Abbott, M (2018) Robot company Starship Technologies plans 1,000 delivery bots, *BBC News*, https://www.bbc.com/news/technology-43949554 (archived at https://perma.cc/H5LE-Q5TF)

11  Moon, M (2017) Dubai tests a passenger drone for its flying taxi service, *Engadget*, https://www.engadget.com/2017/09/26/dubai-volocopter-passenger-drone-test/ (archived at https://perma.cc/6DVY-P3E9)

12  Aerospace Technology (2019) Despite safety concerns drone taxi service will soon become a reality, https://www.aerospace-technology.com/comment/drone-innovation/ (archived at https://perma.cc/A6FL-WQVQ)

13  Rolls-Royce (2018) Rolls-Royce and Finferries demonstrate world's first fully autonomous ferry, https://www.rolls-royce.com/media/press-releases/2018/03-12-2018-rr-and-finferries-demonstrate-worlds-first-fully-autonomous-ferry.aspx (archived at https://perma.cc/KPE9-VNUY)

14  Chatila, R and Tessier, C (2018) A guide to lethal autonomous weapons systems, *CNRS News*, https://news.cnrs.fr/opinions/a-guide-to-lethal-autonomous-weapons-systems (archived at https://perma.cc/PT7B-KAT4)

15  Liptak, A (2019) The US Air Force's jet-powered robotic wingman is like something out of a video game; *The Verge*, https://www.theverge.com/2019/3/9/18255358/us-air-force-xq58-a-valkyrie-prototype-robotic-loyal-wingman-drone-successful-test-flight (archived at https://perma.cc/446W-8MAQ)

16  Sullivan, M (2019) Google says the new Google Glass gives workers 'superpowers', *Fast Company*, https://www.fastcompany.com/90352249/google-says-the-new-google-glass-gives-workers-superpowers (archived at https://perma.cc/S6LQ-KGZQ)

17  Marr, B (2019) The amazing ways John Deere uses AI and Machine Vision to help feed 10 billion people, *Forbes*, https://www.forbes.com/sites/bernardmarr/2019/03/15/the-amazing-ways-john-deere-uses-ai-and-machine-vision-to-help-feed-10-billion-people/#3bfd36042ae9 (archived at https://perma.cc/B5VC-UHFL)

18  Walker, J (2019) Machine learning in manufacturing, *Emerj*, https://emerj.com/ai-sector-overviews/machine-learning-in-manufacturing/ (archived at https://perma.cc/5KJB-HBKC)

19  Marr, B (2017) Internet of Things and machine learning: ever wondered what machines are saying to each other? *Forbes*, https://www.forbes.com/sites/bernardmarr/2017/02/21/how-ai-and-real-time-machine-data-helps-kone-move-millions-of-people-a-day/#91ed4b45f973 (archived at https://perma.cc/9D2H-G4AS)

20  O'Hear, S (2018) HyperSurfaces turns any surface into a user interface using vibration sensors and AI, *Techcrunch*, https://techcrunch.com/2018/11/20/hypersurfaces/ (archived at https://perma.cc/DE48-Z2GR)

21  Marr, B (2019) *Artificial Intelligence in Practice*, Wiley

22  Catapult (nd) 1999-Present: A history of elite wearable technology in team sport, https://www.catapultsports.com/blog/history-elite-wearable-technology (archived at https://perma.cc/9MS7-UVBK)

23  TE Connectivity (nd) Sensors in Basketball, https://www.te.com/usa-en/trends/connected-life-health-tech/sensors-in-sports/sensors-in-basketball.html (archived at https://perma.cc/W7DJ-8Y63)

24  Everlast and PIQ, *PIQ*, https://piq.com/boxing#video (archived at https://perma.cc/F5SD-KYAH)

25  Vision Direct (2019) How smart contact lenses could totally change your perspective, https://www.visiondirect.co.uk/blog/smart-contact-lenses (archived at https://perma.cc/D86L-X5CC)

26  The Atlantic (nd) The contact lens that could turn you into a camera, https://www.theatlantic.com/sponsored/vmware-2017/contact-lens/1634/ (archived at https://perma.cc/VVH9-YTR4)

27  Starr, M (2018) A new smart contact lens could monitor the glucose in your tears in real-time, *Science Alert*, https://www.sciencealert.com/smart-flexible-contact-lens-monitors-glucose-real-time-diabetes (archived at https://perma.cc/LJ9Y-MH3D)

28  Sennaar, K (2019) AI in Medical Devices, *Emerj*, https://emerj.com/ai-sector-overviews/ai-medical-devices-three-emerging-industry-applications/ (archived at https://perma.cc/PX2J-4553)

# CHAPTER FIVE

# Using AI to provide more intelligent services

I ntelligent, AI-enhanced services may mean AI itself becomes the service offering (see 'AI as a service' later in the chapter), or it may mean AI is used to improve what you do for customers, or it may mean AI provides opportunities to develop entirely new services and business models. All three scenarios have one thing in common: AI is a driving factor for business success.

This chapter will contain lots of practical examples that show how businesses use AI to provide more intelligent services. As is to be expected, some of the best examples come from the tech world, from big-budget tech corporations like Amazon. But, as you'll see in this chapter, there are also plenty of examples from other walks of life, far beyond the reaches of Shenzhen or Silicon Valley.

## Why your services need to get smarter

Whether your company is already a service-based business, or you're considering branching from products into services (because, as we saw in Chapter 4, smart products can often open new doors to smart services), AI is crucial to delivering the sort of service your customers want and need. Thanks to data and AI, companies can now develop a better understanding of their customers than ever before – companies have the ability to track customers, see what they're actually doing, understand how they're engaging with a product or service, and so on. Armed with this knowledge, businesses can design much more responsive, personalized solutions and deliver more intelligent, customized services.

The ability to customize your service offering is key, and you'll notice that personalization is a theme that crops up constantly throughout this chapter. If your customers and clients don't already expect a more personalized service offering, take it from me, they soon will do. Businesses that aren't able to offer more intelligent, personalized services risk being left behind – particularly when stiff competition is coming from the tech sector. (See the rise in personal finance apps, which are moving into traditional banking territory, later in this chapter.)

## Taking a leaf out of the tech world's book

It stands to reason that some of the most powerful examples of AI-enhanced services come from the tech world. Let's look at some of the ways that tech companies are using AI to provide more intelligent, thoughtful and personalized services to their users and customers. After all, where the tech world goes, other industries follow – meaning these approaches are rapidly becoming par for the course for all sorts of other businesses. What's more, in many cases, tech-based startups are beginning to step on the toes of more traditional industries, like banking and healthcare. But more on that later in the chapter.

### Amazon's personalized customer recommendations

At Amazon, the entire company is organized around its AI capabilities. Placing AI at the core of all business activities – ie it's not just 'an IT thing' – has paid massive dividends for Amazon, and is something all organizations can and should learn from (read more about building an AI culture in Chapter 8). AI informs Amazon products like Alexa, but it also powers the site's incredibly advanced customer recommendation engine.

Amazon sets the standard in providing a more personalized online shopping experience for its customers, and was one of the first to provide data-driven customer recommendations on what people might like to buy next – based on data such as purchase history (and the purchase history of other similar customers), browsing history, demographics, and items that are commonly bought together. The company's AI recommendation engine is so effective, it generates 35 per cent of the company's revenue.[1]

## Personalized news and video feeds from ByteDance

ByteDance is the company behind TikTok – a video sharing app beloved by kids, and at the time of writing the world's most downloaded app[2] – and Toutiao – a cross between a search engine and a social media platform that delivers a continuous and personalized stream of content to hundreds of millions of users every day.[3]

What's special about both these platforms is that, unlike services like Facebook and Instagram, you don't have to 'like' anything; the AI simply learns your preferences and interests by tracking what you watch and read (and how long you spend watching or reading those items). It then provides more of the same sort of content. The idea is that your entire content feed is customized perfectly for you – and, crucially, you only see the kind of content you really want to see, instead of a feed populated with random, sometimes uninteresting things that your friends and family have 'liked'. (Farewell, cousin Phil's conspiracy theory links!)

## How Netflix surfaces the kind of content we want to watch

Like Amazon, Netflix is a master of the personalized recommendation. Enjoyed Series A? You might like to watch Series B next. This is all based on Netflix's AI, which crunches through masses of data on what users watch, and compares it to the viewing habits of other users with similar profiles. It's all part of Netflix's drive to get users spending more and more time streaming content through the platform. And as part of that drive, the company builds up an incredibly detailed profile of each individual user and indexes that user against hundreds (or maybe even thousands) of different attributes.[4]

Interestingly, it also uses AI to personalize the image thumbnails – stills from the TV show or movie that viewers see when browsing content – to each user profile. Back when you bought a DVD (remember those days?) the DVD case would have an image from the movie on the cover. Now, Netflix has multiple images to choose from to represent a TV show or movie – and the image it shows you is based on what it knows about you as a viewer. Say, for example, you watch a lot of movies with Robert De Niro in. Netflix could show you a movie thumbnail with Robert De Niro in the image, even if he's only got a tiny part in that movie. It's all geared towards getting your attention, and increasing the chances of you clicking, watching and enjoying the content.

Plus, thanks to the enormous amount of data Netflix has on its users' viewing preferences, the company has become a content creator, producing smash hits like *Stranger Things* based on what it knows people love to watch.

## Spotify and personalized music

Spotify is the largest on-demand music streaming service in the world, and this is largely thanks to its use of AI. One of the many ways Spotify personalizes entertainment is via its Discover Weekly feature, which gives users a personalized playlist every week filled with music they haven't yet played on Spotify but are likely to enjoy. It's basically creating a mix tape for you (my kids wouldn't know what I am talking about here).

But the personalization doesn't stop there. In fact, many have speculated that Spotify is keen to move into personalized music composition – where music is created by Spotify AI, rather than by artists and labels (speculation fuelled by the fact that the Spotify team includes François Pachet, a French scientist and expert on music composed by AI[5]). Spotify has already launched a feature called AI Duet, where users can create a duet with a computer.

This potential move into automated, AI-driven music creation (whether it's by Spotify or another provider) could be a game-changer. I predict that, in the not-too-distant future, a whole range of services – from the music we listen to, to the news we read, to the sports highlights we watch – will be created automatically for us by AI rather than humans. Read more about automated content creation in Chapter 6.

## AI as a service

You might be reading these tech-focused examples and wondering how on earth a regular company (ie one without the skills and budget of, say, Amazon) could possibly implement this sort of thing. The answer lies in AI as a service (AIaaS).

AI leaders like Amazon, Microsoft, Baidu, Google, IBM, Alibaba and so on are capitalizing on this rise of AI-driven services and packaging their technology for paying businesses. In other words, you can, through a company like Google, pay for access to the AI technology and capabilities you need, without having to hire in-house data scientists or invest in expensive infrastructure. If you've got the data, you can use an AI service provider like Amazon or IBM to interrogate that data to make your products and services more intelligent. This means even small businesses can benefit from really advanced AI technology – the sort of stuff that was previously only available to tech firms with huge budgets. Read more about AIaaS and how to implement AI in Part Three.

## Other intelligent services in action

Now let's turn to examples from outside the tech world. Here, I want to highlight how AI is helping all sorts of businesses, across a wide range of industries, deliver more intelligent services to their customers.

### Intelligent insurance

Really, insurance spans both services and products, yet I wanted to include it within the services chapter because I believe the most successful insurers of the future will be those that are able to develop a meaningful, value-adding service relationship with their customers. Insurance will shift away from being a transactional product that people buy (and, all being well, rarely use) towards a service that supports customers and genuinely makes their lives easier, healthier, and so on.

Health and life insurance provider Vitality Health is one company that's already making this shift and developing a deeper relationship with its customers. Rather than paying for sickness, as traditional health insurance providers do, Vitality pays for wellness. The company uses data and AI to track and reward customers' healthy behaviour. The idea is to create a shared value system whereby customers benefit from value-added services (and, of course, healthier lives) – while the insurer benefits from lower healthcare costs. Vitality starts by assessing a new member's baseline health and lifestyle information – smoking, drinking, height, blood pressure, etc – and this information is used to determine the customer's Vitality Age. (Interestingly, 79 per cent of people surveyed have a higher Vitality Age than their biological age.[6]) Then, Vitality creates what it calls a Personal Pathway for each member – essentially a plan to improve their Vitality Age by making healthier choices, and rewarding them with discounted services when they stick to the plan. To support this process, Vitality gathers data from compatible wearable technologies, like the Apple Watch, and collects data from partners, including gyms and retailers. So, for example, members earn points for how many steps they take each day, or how healthy their food choices are, and these points can be redeemed against discounted services that support a healthier lifestyle. The healthier your lifestyle, the bigger the rewards. And from Vitality's perspective, they can use the data gathered to price policies more accurately and adjust premiums based on how engaged a member is with their personal programme.

Examples like this show how technology delivers exciting opportunities for insurance companies to offer a more personalized service, better understand their customers, offer better price policies, lower costs, and solve their customers' problems. Another brilliant example of this is the LeakBot tool, a small, clip-on leak detector that can identify hidden leaks on a mains water system before they turn into a bigger, more expensive problem – saving customers and insurers a whole lot of hassle and money.[7] Because the device is so small and relatively inexpensive, insurance companies can easily supply it to customers free of charge – and reap the benefits of preventing expensive water damage claims.

Personally, this is exactly the sort of thing I want from my insurance providers – I want insurance companies to add value, be more proactive, solve problems before they occur, and help me save money. In the future, I think technology-based value-added insurance is a norm we can all look forward to.

### Intelligent financial services

Financial services is an industry I work with a lot and I think it's fair to say there's a certain amount of industry blindness when it comes to introducing more intelligent services, particularly in personal banking; a notable few banking providers are way ahead of the curve, while most others focus only on what their direct banking competitors are doing, without noticing the wave of non-traditional AI-based services moving into their territory.

The truth is, people want more from their banks these days. Every customer wants a more personalized service – the kind of attention that has traditionally been reserved for high net worth customers only. AI enables this kind of mass personalization, automatically delivering insights that help customers better manage their money and achieve their financial goals. If traditional banks can't deliver on personalization, then customers will look elsewhere.

Indeed, they already are, and a wave of tools have come onto the market promising to help people manage their finances and deliver their goals. Chatbot-based services like Cleo and Plum analyse your spending habits, work out how much you can afford to save, and can even funnel money directly from your bank account to a separate fund to keep it safe for a rainy day. While there's still some consumer scepticism about these app services (who wouldn't be wary about sharing their bank login details with someone other than their bank?), it's only a matter of time before these services become mainstream, fully regulated and trusted parts of the financial industry – indeed, many of the available personal finance apps are already regulated by institutions such as the UK's Financial Conduct Authority.

Turning to traditional banks, Royal Bank of Canada is one example of a forward-thinking provider designing more intelligent services for customers. Its banking app uses AI to automatically analyse and categorize spending habits, recommend a personalized monthly budget across areas like 'shopping', 'dining' and 'transportation', and provide notifications that help keep users within budget.

## Intelligent maintenance

In Chapter 4, I mentioned how elevator and escalator company KONE has been introducing sensors into more than one million lifts around the world to monitor how machinery is working and better manage lift maintenance. The real-time data gathered from these sensors includes everything from start and stop times, to acceleration, temperature, noise levels and vibrations running through the cables. Coupled with AI analytics, all this data helps KONE deliver a better maintenance service to customers (read more about this notion of 'predictive maintenance' in Chapter 6), but it's also led to an entirely new business opportunity for the Finnish company. In 2017, KONE announced it would package the data and provide it to customers (ie lift and elevator operators around the world) under the name 24/7 Connected Services.[8]

## Intelligent transport services

In Chapter 4, I talked a lot about how, as a product, cars are becoming more intelligent and automated. Here, I want to talk about the notion of transport 'as a service'.

Fundamentally, the way in which we use cars is changing. It used to be that we would buy a car – a big investment – and keep it until it was necessary to buy a newer one. Cars were a bit like washing machines in that sense. Gradually, the leasing model has become more and more common, whereby a customer makes a monthly payment for, say, two years, and at the end of that period, takes out a new agreement and gets a new car. Now, even that model is starting to look outdated, particularly in urban areas where many people travel to work using public transport and, if they have a car at all, they might only use it in their spare time. Paying a monthly payment for a car that sits idle more than half the time? It's crazy when you think about it.

Increasingly, people want the ability to drive or catch a ride somewhere, whenever and wherever they need, without the hassle and expense of 'owning' a car full-time. This need is being fulfilled through intelligent, AI-fuelled services. Sure, the option to hail a ride has always been there with old-school cab firms, but companies like Uber and, in China, Didi Chuxing have revolutionized this service, using technology to detect where customers are, automate the whole payment side (including the introduction of dynamic, adaptive pricing), and implement a ratings system for drivers and passengers. They're offering a highly improved, much more intelligent service.

Didi Chuxing might not be a household name (yet), but it is in fact the world's largest ride-sharing company. The company, which is absolutely reliant on AI, uses the technology in some really interesting ways to deliver a slick service. For example, it uses AI to tackle traffic congestion and plan more efficient routes; it uses facial recognition technology to confirm driver and passenger identities; and it has an app-based augmented reality (AR, see Chapter 2) navigation feature that helps customers find their way through buildings (such as large train stations) to reach their pick-up location. Plus, in response to a safety backlash in China after the high-profile murders of two Didi passengers, Didi is also implementing new high-tech security features like biometric ID testing and an in-app SOS button that connects directly to the police.

The reason I mention Didi (which is, after all, a tech startup) in this section is because the company is in talks with Nissan to create an electric vehicle ride-sharing service, demonstrating how even traditional auto companies are keen to get in on the transport-as-a-service act.[9] Likewise, Volkswagen is looking at ways to create its own transport-as-a-service offering[10] and, in 2016, Toyota invested in car-lending app Getaround (which is like Airbnb, but for cars).[11] These car manufacturers are looking for AI-driven ways to diversify their business, add new revenue streams, and meet changing market expectations.

### Intelligent fashion and retail

Combining human stylists with the power of AI, Stitch Fix is a great example of how any industry can harness AI to deliver smart, personalized services. The company aims to eliminate the things most of us hate about shopping for clothes – rushing around crowded shopping centres, queueing for changing rooms, discovering an item that looks great on the model looks awful on you, ordering items online only to find they don't fit – by delivering hand-picked clothing to your front door.

How does it work? Users detail their size, style preferences and lifestyle in a questionnaire (they can also link to their Pinterest account). Then, using AI, the system pre-selects clothes that will fit and suit the customer, and a (human) personal stylist chooses the best options from that pre-selected list. And voila, the perfect clothes for you arrive at your door every month. If you don't like or need an item, you simply return it, and the system learns more about what you do and don't want for the future. Plus, using the data Stitch Fix collects from its 3 million active users,[12] the company is also designing its own styles, based on what it knows about its customers' fashion preferences. [13]

It's clear that Stitch Fix has tapped into a consumer desire for smarter shopping (if eliminating the need to spend Saturday afternoons in a department store isn't a great use of AI, then I don't know what is!); no wonder, then, that companies like Amazon and Trunk Club are piling into the same market.

### Intelligent fan engagement

Formula E is at the forefront of using AI to engage its fans. In 2019, Formula E launched a new 'ghost racing' mobile video game that lets fans participate in races in real time – thanks to AR (see Chapter 2). In other words, through your phone, you can get involved in the race in real time, and drive your virtual race car in between the actual racing drivers. The game mimics the exact speed, location and movements of the real cars in the race – meaning the fans playing along at home are competing not against an algorithm or other players, but the real-life racing drivers driving on the track at that moment.[14] If you like motor racing, you should give the game a try – it's an incredibly clever, totally immersive way to deepen the connection between fans and racing, and I wouldn't be at all surprised to see most sports organizations and teams develop similar engagement tools in future.

In fact, AR-based engagement is an idea that could be applied to many more industries, not just sports. Taking a test drive in your dream car. Checking out the facilities at an exclusive new gym. Joining a politician on stage at a political rally. The possibilities for engaging fans, customers, clients, brand advocates and so on is endless.

Motor racing may be exciting, but if there's one sporting event I really love it's Wimbledon. As I write this chapter, I've just had the privilege of attending the 2019 tournament. But for those who aren't lucky enough to be there in the flesh, IBM's Watson AI engine makes sure fans don't miss out on the action. Watson analyses live footage of matches, including player gestures and reactions from the crowd, to automatically compile the perfect match highlights. The system trawls through thousands of hours of footage, as it happens, across the many courts, to create highlights for fans.[15]

## Intelligent healthcare

From the examples given already in this book, it's clear that the healthcare industry is being positively disrupted by technology. My hope is that AI will help to make healthcare universally affordable and accessible to everyone who needs it.

Services like Babylon Health are paving the way for this. The company is confident the diagnostic abilities of its AI are 'on-par with human doctors', after the system scored an impressive 81 per cent on its first attempt at the Membership of the Royal College of General Practitioners exam – the final exam for GPs in training.[16] (In case you're wondering, the average pass mark for the exam is 72 per cent.) In an interview with *Digital Health News*, the founder and chief executive of Babylon Health,

Ali Parsa, said even he was surprised by how fast the AI learned to diagnose a range of health conditions. Going forward, the company is looking at incorporating facial recognition and voice analysis technology to help assess patients in more detail – for example, how much pain a patient is in, or even whether their symptoms are genuine. The company has already signed deals with companies like Tencent and Samsung to help expand the use of the technology.

In parts of the world where affordable healthcare isn't available to the masses, we could see services like this step in to bridge the gap and help patients receive a diagnosis and find a way forward. With the support of companies like Samsung, it's certainly possible that AI-driven healthcare will become much more mainstream.

## Intelligent education

As a parent and a school governor, education is an area that I'm obviously passionate about, and it's exciting to see how AI is being used to improve learning at every stage of our lives – from school to university to workplace training.

Learning has rapidly become a lifelong experience. Gone are the days of learning being the domain of school, college and university students; today, for most people, learning will continue for their whole working lives. Almost nobody has a job for life these days. We're constantly expected to upskill, expand our knowledge, take on more responsibility, adapt to changing markets and work environments, and so on.

Part of delivering more intelligent education is facilitating this idea of lifelong learning – making it easier for people to learn whenever and wherever they need to, and in a way that works for them, through personalized learning solutions. The rise of MOOCS (Massive Online Open Courses) is perhaps the best-known example of this in action. In the workplace, personalized online learning solutions, like those provided by Netex, allow employers to design customized courses for employees, helping them master new skills in a way that works for them. Many of the flexible, adaptive learning solutions available today include innovative technologies like AR and VR (see Chapter 2) and gamification.

Outside of work, plenty of us are passionate about lifelong learning – for example, learning a second language – and there are many intelligent services designed to help us achieve our learning goals. The Duolingo language app is one of my favourite examples of how AI is disrupting lifelong learning. Since it launched in 2011, Duolingo has grown to become the largest language learning platform in the world, and one of the most popular education apps.[17] AI is central to Duolingo's offering. For example, AI is used to work out which level to place new learners at – so they don't feel overwhelmed by the content they're given, but feel challenged and interested enough to keep using the app. The placement test is adaptive and responsive, automatically adjusting the difficulty of questions based on how the user is responding.

Another key part of intelligent education is preparing those in full-time education (whether it's school-age children or university students) for a lifetime of learning, by complementing traditional classroom teaching with technology solutions that monitor how each pupil is progressing in detail, dynamically adjusting the content and delivery to suit each pupil, and providing a more personalized learning experience. Smart content is one aspect of this, where traditional content like textbooks is transformed into more digestible formats and dynamic tools like quizzes – Cram101 being a good example. Then you have intelligent learning platforms where the tutoring is customized to the learning styles and preferences of each individual pupil. For example, Carnegie Learning's Mika software uses AI to provide personalized tutoring and feedback.

## Intelligent matchmaking

As the examples across this chapter and Chapter 4 show, AI now touches almost every aspect of our lives – and finding love is no different. With online dating services and apps, machines build a picture of what you find attractive and make recommendations based on that understanding. They weed out the unsuitable matches for you, in other words, so you (in theory) go on fewer disastrous dates. And this has worked remarkably well so far – more than a million babies have been born to people who met on Match.com.[18]

The trouble is, the technology is only as good as the info it's given – and the thing about love is, a lot of the time, we don't know what we're looking for, or what's good for us! Not to mention the fact that there are plenty of unscrupulous people out there who deliberately lie on their profiles.

A new wave of dating services are using AI to overcome these obstacles and make online dating even more intelligent. With AI, apps have the ability to tailor your matches based on your actions, rather than what you *say* you like. Loveflutter is one such example, using AI to match people based on what it learns about their personality from Twitter. Similarly, voice-activated dating app AIMM gets to know you by asking questions for a week before it recommends matches – it even plays audio snippets of your match describing their perfect date or telling a funny anecdote. And if both parties are happy to chat, AIMM sets up the call.

AI is also helping to spot those who lie in their profiles and pictures. Tantan (China's version of Tinder) uses AI to spot when users have excessively touched up their profile pics.[19] AI is also being used to identify dating scammers who trick people into handing over cash – Brits lost an alarming £50 million to dating scammers in 2018 – and one neural network was able to spot scammers and fakes with 93 per cent accuracy.[20]

---

**KEY TAKEAWAYS**

In this chapter we've learned:

- The most successful service providers of the future will be those that can use data and AI to provide a more thoughtful, intelligent and personalized service to their customers. If you ignore AI as a means to enhance your service offering, you risk being seriously left behind.

- AI provides an incredible opportunity to really get to know your customers – what they like, what they don't like, what they *actually* do (as opposed to what they *say* they do), how they engage with your service, what's most likely to get them to engage more deeply or for longer periods of time, and so on.

- AI-driven services are no longer the sole domain of big tech firms. Thanks to AI as a service, any business can benefit from AI technology to deliver a more intelligent service to its customers.

---

In order to provide more intelligent, AI-enhanced services, you may need to improve, automate or overhaul some of your business operations. Turn the page to read some incredible examples of how companies are using AI to enhance their internal business processes.

## Endnotes

1 MacKensey, S *et al* (2013) How retailers can keep up with consumers, *McKinsey*, https://www.mckinsey.com/industries/retail/our-insights/how-retailers-can-keep-up-with-consumers (archived at https://perma.cc/X8GY-MY4Q)

2 Business Today (2019) TikTok overtakes Facebook as most downloaded app, https://www.businesstoday.in/latest/trends/tiktok-most-downloaded-app/story/346435.html (archived at https://perma.cc/N8ZT-4MAY)

3 Byford, S (2018) TikTok owner ByteDance is now the world's most valuable startup, *The Verge*, https://www.theverge.com/2018/10/26/18026250/bytedance-china-tiktok-valuation-highest-toutiao (archived at https://perma.cc/L3M7-2F89)

4 Yu, A (2019) How Netflix uses AI, data science, and machine learning – from a product perspective, *Medium*, https://becominghuman.ai/how-netflix-uses-ai-and-machine-learning-a087614630fe (archived at https://perma.cc/QW52-FJ2S)

5 Marr, B (2017) The amazing ways Spotify uses Big Data, AI and machine learning to drive business success, *Forbes*, https://www.forbes.com/sites/bernardmarr/2017/10/30/the-amazing-ways-spotify-uses-big-data-ai-and-machine-learning-to-drive-business-success/#72ef64ee4bd2 (archived at https://perma.cc/F7YR-K5CN)

6 EIO (2018) Vitality: A data-driven approach to better health, *Digital Initiative*, https://digital.hbs.edu/platform-digit/submission/vitality-a-data-driven-approach-to-better-health/ (archived at https://perma.cc/5XEP-TGQW)

7 LeakBot, https://leakbot.io/ (archived at https://perma.cc/WDC7-4CFK)

8 Marr, B (2017) Internet of Things and machine learning: ever wondered what machines are saying to each other? *Forbes*, https://www.forbes.com/sites/bernardmarr/2017/02/21/how-ai-and-real-time-machine-data-helps-kone-move-millions-of-people-a-day/#91ed4b45f973 (archived at https://perma.cc/9MRE-DUWQ)

9 Hanley, S (2019) Didi Chuxing proposes joint venture with Nissan & Dongfeng, seeks capital injection from SoftBank, *Clean Technica*, https://cleantechnica.com/2019/07/02/didi-chuxing-proposes-joint-venture-with-nissan-dongfeng-seeks-capital-injection-from-softbank/ (archived at https://perma.cc/V4YJ-U7C8)

10 #2 Platform Business Model – Mobility As A Service, https://platformbusinessmodel.com/2-platform-business-news-mobility-service/ (archived at https://perma.cc/K4VV-ZYH7)

11 Etherington, D (2016) Toyota partners with Getaround on car-sharing, *Tech Crunch*, https://techcrunch.com/2016/10/31/toyota-partners-with-getaround-on-car-sharing/ (archived at https://perma.cc/5HT5-97GY)

12 Rocco, M (2019) Stitch Fix surges on user growth and rosier sales figures, *Financial Times*, https://www.ft.com/content/07bb3f6a-4441-11e9-a965-23d669740bfb (archived at https://perma.cc/TJ8P-XE37)

13 Marr, B (2018) Stitch Fix: the amazing use case of using artificial intelligence in fashion retail, *Forbes*, https://www.forbes.com/sites/bernardmarr/2018/05/25/stitch-fix-the-amazing-use-case-of-using-artificial-intelligence-in-fashion-retail/#5823c3d3292b (archived at https://perma.cc/PL75-5PJQ)

14 McCaskill, S (2019) Formula E lets fans race drivers in real time with new mobile game, *Forbes*, https://www.forbes.com/sites/stevemccaskill/2019/04/30/formula-e-lets-fans-race-

drivers-in-real-time-with-new-mobile-game/#a4320c6301ba (archived at https://perma.cc/
6PM6-Z9BT)

15  IBM (nd) AI highlights with IBM Watson, https://www.ibm.com/marketing/uk-en/
wimbledon/?cm_mmc=OSocial_Socialhub-_-Hybrid+Cloud_IBM+Cloud-_-IUK_IUK-_-
OSocial+Wimbledon+Influencer+Drive+to+lp+BM&cm_mmca1=000036XS&cm_
mmca2=10011297 (archived at https://perma.cc/6ZXY-NJT5)

16  Hughes, O (2018) Babylon Health says AI abilities 'on par with human doctors',
*Digital Health*, https://www.digitalhealth.net/2018/07/babylon-ai-abilities-on-par-
human-doctors/ (archived at https://perma.cc/Z57W-9RK8)

17  Gagliordi, N (2019) How Duolingo uses AI to disrupt the language learning market,
*ZDNet*, https://www.zdnet.com/article/how-duolingo-uses-ai-to-disrupt-the-language-
learning-market/ (archived at https://perma.cc/G5HX-XBYA)

18  Ghafourifar, A (2017) How AI can help you find a date, *Venture Beat*,
https://venturebeat.com/2017/01/11/how-ai-can-help-you-find-a-date/ (archived at
https://perma.cc/B7PQ-XJNV)

19  China's Tinder embraces AI as it eyes growth from the country's singles; *South China
Morning Post*, https://www.scmp.com/tech/china-tech/article/2154856/chinas-tinder-
embraces-ai-it-eyes-growth-countrys-singles (archived at https://perma.cc/U3AP-RNW2)

20  Tao, L and Deng, I (2018) Dating app scammers spotted by AI, *BBC News*,
https://www.bbc.co.uk/news/technology-48472811 (archived at https://perma.cc/
E5L5-6FEY)

# CHAPTER SIX

# Using AI to improve your business operations and processes

Like many companies, you may be looking to make your business more efficient, more streamlined, and better positioned to deliver success, grow and meet changing market needs. AI helps organizations do all this and more.

This chapter contains lots of practical examples that show how a vast array of businesses are already using AI to create more intelligent business processes. In many cases, this means switching to more automated business processes; from detecting fraud to hiring the best employees, business processes are becoming increasingly automated. But, as you'll see in this chapter, automation doesn't have to mean investing in an army of robot workers and making hundreds or thousands of humans redundant. In fact, AI-enhanced business operations often mean using AI to augment the work of humans, or structure workflows to get the best out of both humans and machines.

The need for improved business processes may spin out of your company's move towards more intelligent products or services – as shown in Chapters 4 and 5 – or you may simply need your organization to be more competitive. Whatever the underlying reasons, I hope this chapter will inspire and encourage you on the road to improving your business processes through AI.

## Why apply AI to your business operations and processes?

AI offers immense opportunities to improve business processes in a number of ways, such as:

- reducing costs;
- automating and streamlining core business activities;
- freeing up valuable employees to focus on more creative activities that drive business success, as opposed to mundane, repetitive activities;
- improving customer satisfaction;
- driving increased sales and revenue.

As an example of the potential benefits that are out there for the taking, let's look at one company that's using AI in many different ways across the organization. You might be expecting me to namecheck Google, Amazon or another big tech firm here, but in fact I want to highlight PepsiCo, the company behind brands such as Pepsi, Gatorade and Lipton. This snack and beverage producer is a shining example of using AI, data and analytics to improve performance across the business.

For example, PepsiCo subsidiary Frito-Lay uses machine learning (see Chapter 2) to enhance the manufacturing process for potato chips. One project automates the quality control process for chips by effectively firing lasers at chips and listening to the sounds generated – AI algorithms analyse the sounds to determine the chips' texture and quality. From there, machine learning and machine vision (see Chapter 2) was used to develop a system able to predict the weight of potatoes being processed – meaning the company no longer had to spend $300,000 per line on weighing elements. At 35 lines in the United States alone, that's a considerable saving.[1] Another cost-saving project in the works will assess the 'per cent peel' of potatoes after they've been through the peeling process – estimated to save around $1 million a year in the United States.

PepsiCo has also used AI to help hire candidates. It has deployed Robot Vera (developed by Russian startup Stafory) to conduct phone interviews with candidates for sales positions, and used the technology to quickly fill 250 factory vacancies in Russia. Vera can interview 1,500 candidates in just nine hours – something that would take human recruiters nine weeks.

PepsiCo also has its own in-house technology platform, Ada, which combines human insight with algorithms. Ada can pull together data from a variety of sources to allow PepsiCo to better leverage the massive amounts of data it collects from operations, and is expected to be used to enhance decision making in design, research and pricing, to name just a few applications.

The company has also used AI social prediction tools to aggregate publicly available consumer conversations to identify potential new product opportunities. Plus, it uses an analytics platform called Pep Worx to advise retail stores on the best items to stock, where to place them and what promotions to use. For example, when the company was launching Quaker Overnight Oats, it used analytics to identify 24 million households that it felt it would be appropriate to market to. Then, PepsiCo identified the shopping venues most likely to be visited by these households and created promotions in those venues targeted to that audience – helping to drive 80 per cent of the product's sales growth in the first 12 months after launch.

PepsiCo's wide-ranging use of AI shows us the importance of developing an AI culture in your business. If the entire company is convinced of and excited about the benefits of AI, you stand a much better chance of adopting AI successfully and delivering real business benefits. Read more about the people and culture side of AI in Chapter 8.

## Starting with robotic process automation

Across every industry, companies are feeling the pressure to increase efficiencies and performance while reducing costs. For many, robotic process automation (RPA) provides a solution to this problem.

RPA is a huge topic right now and is only set to get bigger. In fact, according to leading research and consultancy company Gartner, spending on RPA technology will reach $2.4 billion by 2022. Sounds impressive, but what exactly is RPA? In a nutshell, RPA means using computers to automate parts of our processes – particularly the repetitive, mundane, structured tasks that human workers spend time on every day. The idea is, with machines taking care of the more mundane processes, human workers can focus on higher-level, more valuable and more creative activities.

For those who think RPA is far beyond them in terms of budget and expertise, robots as a service (RaaS) is a fast-emerging area that lets businesses deploy RPA as a cloud-based service – meaning you effectively hire bots rather than invest in expensive back-end infrastructure, and scale operations up and down as needed. In one example, Cobalt Robotics offers an RaaS security platform that's 65 per cent cheaper than human security guards.[2] You could, therefore, have one human managing a remote team of robots, instead of paying for a five-person security team – with the added bonus of collecting increased data and insights for security optimization.

## Other examples of RPA at work

The financial industry was an early adopter of RPA, but now a wide range of industries are using RPA technology for tasks such as communicating with other digital systems, capturing data, retrieving information, processing transactions, and more. Across tasks like this, RPA reduces labour costs and eliminates human error. For example, a large banking provider used 85 software bots to run 13 processes that handled 1.5 million requests in a year – capacity that equalled 230 full-time employees at around 30 per cent of the cost.[3] What's more, the number of tasks completed 'right first time' increased.

Other examples of RPA in action include:

- **Call centre operations and customer queries**
  Many customer requests can be supported by RPA technology, and this can be particularly effective when combined with chatbot technology.
- **Transferring paper records to digital**
  An RPA solution can read documents and forms and enter data into the new system, without introducing human error.
- **Inputting and processing insurance claims**
  RPA tools can do this faster than humans, and with fewer errors.
- **Automating help desk responses**
  For straightforward, repetitive issues, RPA can be used to address users' technical problems and queries, freeing up the human support staff for other tasks.
- **Credit card applications**
  RPA is behind the majority of credit card applications these days. Bots can be programmed to easily handle all aspects of the process, including doing credit checks and deciding whether to accept or reject the application.
- **HR onboarding**
  RPA can augment many of the more repetitive HR tasks. For example, when a manager has chosen their new hire, automated bots can take

over tasks such as issuing the formal job offer letter, archiving the application forms and CVs of non-successful candidates, creating a new IT account and logins, and generating an ID card.

- **Sales and marketing**
Both sales and marketing are full of repetitive tasks, often involving multiple computer systems. RPA bots can, for example, enter new customer or lead information into CRM systems, check data consistency across different systems, conduct continuous competitor research and perform social listening tasks to gain a better understanding of customers. Again, RPA bots combined with intelligent chatbots can be particularly effective in a sales and marketing context. More on chatbots coming up later in the chapter.

### So is RPA the same as AI?

Sort of, but not quite. While automation is often a key aim of AI, RPA works slightly differently. Crucially, the RPA bots have to be programmed to complete a task, while AI systems can typically learn and decide for themselves how best to complete a task. In other words, you can have RPA without AI, and you can have AI without RPA. However, the two complement each other very nicely – consider the benefits of combining RPA with an AI technique such as machine learning, which enables the RPA bots to learn and get better at repetitive tasks. In this way, for many companies, RPA is often a stepping stone to adopting more advanced AI further down the road.

### Real-world examples of AI-enhanced business functions

As with AI-enhanced products (Chapter 4) and services (Chapter 5), I want to use the bulk of this chapter to showcase real-life examples of companies using AI to improve their internal processes. Here, my intention is to demonstrate a range of common operational functions across various industries. But it was impossible to include every facet of typical business operations – the chapter would have been 10 times longer than it is! So if you don't see your particular departmental focus or expertise represented in this chapter, that certainly doesn't mean AI doesn't apply to your field. Across any function, in any industry, there's the potential to streamline or automate operations or processes through AI. These examples provide just a taste of what's possible.

## Wasting less time on meetings

If this seems a surprising place to start, consider this: in the United States alone, employees attend around 62 meetings a month. The average middle manager spends around 35 per cent of his or her time in meetings; and those decision makers higher up in the organization may spend as much as 50 per cent of their time in meetings.[4] That's *a lot* of organizational time taken up in meetings, let alone the time taken to schedule and organize those meetings, make and circulate notes, and tick off all the follow-up actions. When you factor in the additional admin involved, a one-hour meeting can cost significantly more of people's time. Yet, for an activity that sucks up so much time, meetings are notoriously unproductive; some figures suggest 37 per cent of meetings add no value to the organization.[5]

AI may not be able to eliminate meetings altogether, but it can at least cut down the amount of admin involved before, during and after the event. Voice assistant platforms like Voicea can listen in on meetings, capture key highlights and actions, and create and share actionable notes afterwards. The Sonia tool does a similar thing, but is designed to capture client calls, transcribing the entire conversation and automatically summarizing key decisions, follow-up items and actions. Because Sonia is designed for client calls, it can also automate CRM entry for compliance.

When combined with other voice assistants such as Google Duplex, which can schedule appointments for you (see Chapter 2), these AI-enabled tools can help to seriously cut down the admin hours that surround meetings, leaving your people free to focus on value-adding activities instead.

## Enhancing sales and marketing processes

The use of chatbots is an obvious example of an AI-driven sales and marketing process, and many household names have been able to drive revenue and grow their audience using chatbots. For example, the UK retailer Marks & Spencer added a virtual digital assistant function to its website to help customers troubleshoot discount codes and other common issues without needing human intervention – and the company says this function has saved online sales worth £2 million that it would otherwise have lost.[6] In another example, British online fashion and cosmetic retailer Asos was able to triple orders and reach 35 per cent more people using Messenger chatbots.[7]

AI can also be used to make market research more intelligent, cost effective and efficient. In fact, 80 per cent of market researchers feel AI will have a positive impact on market research.[8] AI tools can deliver customer insights in near real time, identify and drill down to incredibly specific target audiences, and conduct responsive questionnaires that adapt to the respondent's answers (a bit like the Duolingo language app quiz I mentioned in Chapter 5). Plus, there's far less chance of results being skewed by human bias or errors.

With AI, traditional marketing survey methods can be greatly improved. Take the Net Promoter Score (NPS) method, which asks customers how likely they are to recommend a brand, service or product to others, with the customer answering on a numbered scale. NPS was devised this way to make it easy to analyse and benchmark scores. However, without open-ended, freeform answers, it's missing any real insight on *why* a customer is likely (or not likely) to recommend your offering. With AI analytics, particularly sentiment analysis and natural language processing (NLP, see Chapter 2) such open-ended freeform answers can be quickly and easily mined for information, thus providing much more detailed insight on what customers value and what could be done better. Thanks to AI, it's possible to understand not only the meaning of customer responses, but also the sentiment behind those responses.

Many off-the-peg customer relationship management (CRM) solutions are now routinely incorporating AI analytics, enabling sales teams to automatically generate more valuable insights. For example, Salesforce's Einstein AI technology can predict which customers are most likely to generate more revenue, and which are most likely to take their custom elsewhere. Armed with knowledge like this, the sales team can focus their time where it delivers most value for the business.

### Assessing and improving customer service

Many call centre operations have been automated for a while, but technology company Transcosmos has developed an AI solution that can help companies judge the quality of calls and customer service. According to Transcosmos, customer service quality in call centres comes down to a combination of manners, information given, and delivering additional value. Focusing on these three elements, Transcosmos has developed an AI which automatically judges the quality of service given 'at speed with human accuracy' – and can detect inappropriate and problematic customer service with more than twice the accuracy of a voice recognition system.[9]

## Improving product development processes

For me, this is one of the coolest applications of AI, particularly when it comes to AI and creativity – circle back to the examples of AI creativity in Chapter 2, or check out a clip of AI bringing the Mona Lisa 'to life'.[10] *Generative design* is a cutting-edge field that's spun out of this idea of machines being able to 'create' like humans.

Generative design means augmenting the work of human designers and engineers using intelligent software. With generative design, companies that design and build products can quickly generate multiple designs from a single idea – you simply input your design goals and other requirements and let the software explore all the possible designs that could fulfil those specifications. The software does all the heavy lifting of working out what works and what doesn't, saving many, many hours of time – plus the expense of creating prototypes that don't deliver. Applied across fields like architecture, design, manufacturing and construction, generative design has the potential to transform the design process. In one example, generative design software was used to collaboratively create a new chair design with renowned designer Philippe Starck (he set out his overarching vision and the software took over from there).[11] In another, NASA used generative design to come up with a concept for a spider-like interplanetary lander.[12]

Digital twin technology – essentially, creating an exact digital replica of a physical object – is another transformational development in product design. Digital twins are possible thanks to Internet of Things sensors (IoT, see Chapter 2), which can gather masses of data from things in the physical world – data that can then be reconstructed by machines. If you can create a digital twin of a product, then you can easily access incredible insights on how to make that product better, more efficient, and so on. Using what you learn from the digital twin, you can make improvements to the real-life product with less risk (and expense). General Electric was an early adopter of digital twin technology, and Chevron expects to make huge savings in maintenance using digital twins.[13]

## Automating content generation

In Chapter 2, I outlined how machines are capable of generating text, and how organizations like Forbes, which I write for regularly, are now producing articles with the help of AI. Outside the world of news and media, a variety of organizations need to produce copy on a regular basis – including product descriptions and technical reports.

Multinational ecommerce leader Alibaba has come up with an AI-enabled copywriting tool that's capable of generating more than 20,000 lines of copy in just one second.[14] Called AI-CopyWriter, the tool learns from existing text (for example, a product page on a website) and can automatically generate related copy. It's already been used by retailers and ecommerce businesses such as Esprit, Dickies and Taobao.

In another example, German bank Commerzbank has been using AI to save research time and costs by generating equity research reports. The process isn't completely automated as yet, but the technology is already able to perform about 75 per cent of what a human equity analyst does. Of course, Commerzbank isn't alone in churning out lengthy industry reports – tools like the Quill platform (by Narrative Science) are designed to help organizations produce these reports quickly and easily, and Quill is already being used by companies like Forbes and Groupon.[15]

## Improving the manufacturing process

The use of robots in manufacturing is nothing new. What is new is 'cobots', or collaborative robots. This latest generation of robotic systems is capable of working alongside humans, augmenting what human workers do, and interacting seamlessly (and safely) with the human workforce. Thanks to AI technologies like machine vision, cobots are aware of the humans around them and can react accordingly – for example, by adjusting their speed or reversing to avoid humans and other obstacles – meaning workflows can be designed to get the very best out of both humans and robots. Easy to program, fast to set up and with an average price tag of around $24,000 each,[16] cobots are a viable option to help smaller and mid-sized firms compete with larger manufacturers.

Many companies have been able to increase efficiencies and lower manufacturing costs with cobots. For example, at the Ford Fiesta plant in Cologne, Germany, human workers and cobots work together on the assembly line to install shock absorbers on cars.[17] And in Amazon fulfilment centres, cobots bring shelves of merchandise to human workers to prepare for shipment – helping to reduce the time taken to complete an order from more than one hour to 15 minutes.[18]

Now, we even have robots capable of building other robots. Swiss robotics company ABB is splashing out $150 million on an advanced robotics factory in China that will use robots to build robots.[19]

3D printing is another innovation that's transforming manufacturing, and it's now possible to 3D print all sorts of things – even chocolate and hamburgers.[20] The bodies of electric vehicles and other cars have been 3D printed, as have houses. By combining 3D printing with robotics and AI analytics, manufacturers can deliver even greater efficiencies and cost savings. For example, Autodesk's Netfabb 3D printing software uses machine learning to generate and evaluate digital models for 3D printing production.[21]

Elsewhere in manufacturing, the rise of connected IoT devices is driving increased insights into machine performance, enabling companies to be much more proactive when it comes to maintenance – potentially identifying and solving problems before they occur, in a development known as 'predictive maintenance'. The KONE smart lift and elevators example from Chapter 4 is a brilliant illustration of predictive main-tenance in action. In another example, field service management provider ServiceMax has created an IoT-driven platform called Connected Field Services to help companies switch to a predictive maintenance model. Eventually, ServiceMax hopes the platform will help guarantee 100 per cent uptime availability for mission-critical equipment.[22]

## Enhancing recruitment and other HR processes

Being as people oriented as it is, HR isn't exactly an obvious match with AI. Yet AI is fast finding many uses in HR processes, including recruit-ment. For large employers like Unilever, which recruits around 30,000 people a year and handles 1.8 million applications,[23] finding ways to streamline and improve the time- and resource-heavy recruitment process is essential. Step forward, AI.

Unilever partnered with AI recruitment specialist Pymetrics to create an online platform capable of conducting initial assessments of candi-dates in their own home (useful when you consider applicants come from all over the world). To start with, the candidate plays a selection of games that test their aptitude, logic and reasoning, and appetite for risk. Machine learning algorithms then assess the results to gauge how suitable the candidate is for the role they've applied for, by comparing their profile against those of previously successful employees.

In the second stage of recruitment, the candidate submits a video interview, which is again assessed by machine learning algorithms (looking at factors like the language used and body language) to judge who might be a good fit. According to Unilever, around 70,000 person-hours of interviewing and assessing candidates has been cut thanks to this automated screening of candidates.[24] Candidates that make it through the automated screening stages then progress to meeting human leaders and recruiters from the company.

What's also great about this automated screening system is that it's capable of giving feedback to all unsuccessful applicants – something that would be impossible for human HR personnel to do with so many applicants. With this system, every applicant gets a couple of pages of feedback to help them with future applications.

And for those who make the grade and join Unilever as an employee, the company has implemented an AI chatbot to help new starters get settled in their roles. Called Unabot, and built on Microsoft's Bot framework, the bot uses NLP to understand what employees want to know and fetch the right information for them. Now, Unabot is the 'front face' for any employee question, from how much holiday allowance they have, to the best place to park!

In fact, chatbots are increasingly being used in all sorts of organizations, big and small, to answer straightforward employee questions and even conduct surveys. As an example of an off-the-peg HR chatbot solution, the Polly bot is able to conduct employee surveys and gather employee feedback, allowing businesses to monitor how employees are feeling and nip morale problems in the bud before they escalate.

## Automating IT processes

A range of IT processes can be automated or augmented by AI. Detecting phishing emails is one prominent example. As phishing scams have become more and more sophisticated, so too have the tools to detect and stop scammers. Cybersecurity provider Webroot uses machine learning to improve its detection of phishing scams – designed to route victims to fake websites and get them to part with their bank or credit card details, personal information or login details – and to compile an ever-growing database of illegitimate websites. New phishing scams are constantly emerging and keeping up with new threats would be near-impossible without serious computing power and the analytics power of AI.

Previous training cycles for updating Webroot's phishing models (which identify and stop phishing attempts) used to be between three and five days – meaning the models were updated with new threats once or twice a week. Thanks to machine learning and enormous computing power, that's been cut to three to five hours – meaning the models can now be updated several times a day. This improvement is essential when you consider the company is identifying between 2,000 and 6,000 phishing sites every day.[25]

### Detecting fraud with AI

Mastercard is one of the many organizations using AI to help detect and prevent fraud, while reducing the frustration of customers having a genuine transaction declined. According to research by Mastercard, a third of us have withdrawn our custom from a retailer due to our cards being refused – and the cost to businesses of these so-called 'false declines' is 13 times higher than the cost of actual card fraud.[26] Often when a genuine transaction is declined, it's because it's been mistakenly flagged as fraudulent in some way, but Mastercard is using AI (in particular, predictive analytics and machine learning) to make its fraud detection much more accurate – cutting the rate of false declines by 50 per cent.

Processing 75 billion transactions per year at 45 million global locations, Mastercard is generating a constant stream of data. The decisions on whether or not to decline a transaction are based on self-teaching algorithms that learn from this constant stream of data (as opposed to fixed, preconceived rules, as in traditional methods) to decide whether a transaction is likely to be fraudulent or not. Not only has this helped to drastically cut the rate of false declines, it's also caught billions of dollars' worth of actual fraud.

### Making transport and logistics more efficient

In Chapter 4, we saw how transport-related products such as cars and ships are becoming smarter thanks to AI, and this is delivering efficiencies for a wide range of organizations, from pizza delivery companies to ferry operators.

For me, drone ships and autonomous ferries are a particularly inter-esting area of transport and logistics – although one that receives far less attention than autonomous cars and lorries. While we're still some way from fully autonomous vessels becoming the norm, for those in the business of transporting people and goods on the water, AI-enhanced processes can help to improve safety, increase efficiency and relieve humans from unsafe and repetitive tasks. According to a study by Allianz, between 75 per cent and 96 per cent of maritime accidents are caused by human error,[27] indicating how autonomous ships could make our oceans much safer. What's more, reducing the number of crew can lead to significant savings for shipping providers, not just in terms of salaries but also crew provisions. With crew-related expenses accounting for around 30 per cent of the typical budget, this could make a huge difference to the bottom line.[28]

If your company transports products or components – by sea or other means – it's highly likely part of that journey or process will become automated in some way in the future. For example, Ford has unveiled a two-legged robot that folds up into the back of a self-driving car; when the car reaches its destination, the robot – which is called Digit – unfolds itself out of the boot and completes the last stage of the delivery.[29] Developments like this could revolutionize the process of delivering parcels.

## Improving retail operations

US glasses retailer Warby Parker is a fantastic example of a company using AI to streamline the process of helping customers find the right product. My teenage daughter is a glasses wearer and she naturally wants the latest trendy designer frames – but doesn't necessarily know which shape, style and colour will best suit her. The traditional way around this would be to spend ages in-store on a Saturday morning with a store representative, trying on many, many different frames – while my other children start climbing the walls in boredom. Thankfully, AI has come to the rescue and saved us from this horror. Warby Parker uses AI and augmented reality (AR, see Chapter 2) to help customers 'try on' glasses virtually, via their phone. Using the iPhone X's camera and Apple's Face ID face-scanning capabilities, Warby Parker's app creates a detailed map of the customer's face and is able to recommend the frames best suited to their face shape. The customer can then see a 3D preview of their face 'wearing' the glasses.

Technology like this can transform retail processes, boost sales and, in many cases, reduce customer returns. For example, ecommerce platform WatchBox, which specializes in luxury pre-owned watches, uses an AR-enabled feature in its app to let customers see how the watch they're interested in would look in real life on their wrist. When you consider that around a third of all online purchases are returned, features like this could save retailers a great deal of time, hassle and expense.[30]

Another ecommerce company is reducing returns by using AI to intelligently predict what will be sold within the next 30 days. German company Otto's analysis found that customers are less likely to return items when they arrive within two days and if they get everything they ordered at once, rather than in multiple shipments. However, because (like Amazon) Otto sells products from other brands, stocking and shipping products all at once is a major challenge. To solve this problem, Otto used a deep learning algorithm (see Chapter 2) to analyse 3 billion past transactions and variables such as weather data to predict what customers will want to buy in the next 30 days... with 90 per cent accuracy.[31] Armed with this knowledge, the company can order the right products ahead of time, so that customer orders with multiple items can be shipped all in one go. In fact, this process is done without any human intervention at all – the system automatically orders around 200,000 products a month from third-party providers. The result? Product returns have been reduced by over 2 million items a year. What's more, rather than losing human jobs to automation, the company ended up hiring more workers.

AI is also helping retailers deliver greater efficiencies in-store. Amazon, for example, is using AI (specifically machine vision) to eliminate the checkout process in its growing chain of Amazon Go grocery and convenience stores.[32] The customer simply scans themselves in when they enter the shop (using the Amazon app on their smart phone), picks up what they want from the shelves, then leaves. This is possible because cameras track the customer as they shop, monitor what they take, and then charge the cost automatically to the customer's Amazon account. Imagine that: no queuing at checkouts, no handing over cash and, best of all, no 'unexpected item in the bagging area'!

Walmart is also using computer vision, not to remove checkouts altogether, but to combat 'shrinkage' – loss from theft and scanning errors – at more than 1,000 stores. Known as Missed Scan Detection, the initiative involves using cameras at both self-checkout machines and regular, cashier-manned checkouts to automatically identify when an item hasn't been scanned properly (whether by accident or on purpose). When a missed scan is identified, the system alerts a member of staff. With estimates suggesting shrinkage at Walmart could equate to more than $4 billion a year, technology like this could potentially have a huge impact on the bottom line.[33] So far, so good: shrinkage rates have declined at stores where Missed Scan Detection has been deployed.

## Automating the fast food industry

AI and robotics are making serious waves in the fast food industry, particularly when it comes to food delivery. In Chapter 4 I mentioned how Domino's Pizza has been using delivery robots to make pizza delivery more efficient. California-based Zume Pizza showed us that it is possible to also automate much of the pizza preparation process. Even though the company has since refocused on another part of the business, it proved what's now possible. When a customer placed an order (via the Zume app), a robot called Doughbot got the ball rolling by turning a dough ball into a pizza base in just nine seconds. Then two other robots – named Giorgio and Pepe – applied the sauce to the base. From there, another robot, Marta, spread the sauce evenly over the base. Placing the toppings was still too tricky for the robots to handle – the different sizes and textures of toppings make it difficult to automate – so humans stepped in for this part. Then it was back to robotic colleagues, as robots Bruno and Vincenzo shovelled the pizzas in and out of the oven.[34]

## Picking fruit with robots

While agriculture has been an enthusiastic adopter of AI and robotics, picking tender fruits like raspberries has been the preserve (pardon the pun) of human pickers. Robots just didn't have the tender touch that soft fruits require… until now. The world's first raspberry-picking robot, recently trialled at a farm in West Sussex, UK, could indicate a new, automated future of fruit picking. While a human fruit picker can typically manage around 15,000 fruits in an eight-hour shift, the robot is expected to be able to pick more than 25,000 raspberries a day.[35] Guided by sensors and cameras, the 1.8-metre-tall machine can identify ripe fruit and – gently – pick it using a robotic arm. The fruit then gets placed in a tray, where it's sorted according to maturity, and decanted into punnets ready for transportation. The final version of the robot, which is expected to go into full production this year, will have four robotic arms all picking at the same time – with the ability to pick for up to 20 hours a day. The machine has also been trialled on tomatoes in China.

## Making construction safer

More people die in construction than in any other industry,[36] with falling being a major risk factor on construction sites. But AI is already helping to make construction a safer industry through tools like Autodesk's Construction IQ, which is able to predict when falls and other injuries are likely to happen. Autodesk's data scientists hit upon the idea when trying to find applications for the masses of data collected on modern-day construction sites. (The construction industry has been an enthusiastic adopter of mobile and IoT devices, such as sensors that detect when concrete is ready to use.)

Construction IQ takes data from construction sites – particularly notes created by contractors and subcontractors while on site – and uses NLP to analyse the text, assess risk and warn of potential hazards. Evidence suggests the software is already making construction sites safer; one construction company I spoke to, BAM Ireland, told me that thanks to Autodesk's software they had achieved a 20 per cent reduction in quality and safety issues on site.[37]

---

### KEY TAKEAWAYS

In this chapter we've learned:

- Across a wide range of industries, organizations are using AI to enhance and automate some of their internal business processes, including sales, HR, manufacturing and logistics.

- The benefits of AI-enabled business operations include reduced costs, more efficient processes, better performance, improved sales, and more.

- Enhancing your internal operations through AI doesn't necessarily mean huge investments in technology, infrastructure and expertise. There are many off-the-peg solutions, from Robotic Process Automation (RPA) tools to advanced data analytics tools, that can be deployed in your organization relatively easily.

---

I hope the chapters in this part have convinced you of the merits of using AI to enhance your products, services and business processes, and demonstrated the exciting ways companies are already generating significant improvements, cost savings, customer insights, and more through AI. But how do you translate all this into your own business? Where do you start? How can you create an AI strategy that's appropriate for your company's unique requirements, goals and challenges? That's what Part Three of this book is all about: how to go about transforming your business into an AI business. Up first: how to pinpoint the most valuable AI-related opportunities for your business.

## Endnotes

1   Marr, B (2019) The fascinating ways PepsiCo uses artificial intelligence and machine learning to deliver success, *Forbes*, https://www.forbes.com/sites/bernardmarr/2019/04/05/the-fascinating-ways-pepsico-uses-artificial-intelligence-and-machine-learning-to-deliver-success/#30fad99a311e (archived at https://perma.cc/FM4Y-EQS4)

2   Radfar, H (2019) The rise of robots-as-a-service, *Venture Beat*, https://venturebeat.com/2019/06/30/the-rise-of-robots-as-a-service/ (archived at https://perma.cc/F25G-YR66)

3   Schatsky, S, Muraskin, C and Kaushik, I (2016) Robotic process automation, *Deloitte Insights*, https://www2.deloitte.com/insights/us/en/focus/signals-for-strategists/cognitive-enterprise-robotic-process-automation.html#endnote-sup-2 (archived at https://perma.cc/BCV7-WCVU)

4   Martin (2019) How much time do we spend in meetings (Hint: it's scary), *Cleverism*, https://www.cleverism.com/time-spent-in-meetings/ (archived at https://perma.cc/QSW3-HG9W)

5   Martin (2019) How much time do we spend in meetings (Hint: it's scary), *Cleverism*, https://www.cleverism.com/time-spent-in-meetings/ (archived at https://perma.cc/QSW3-HG9W)

6   Joseph, S (2018) A year in, Marks & Spencer's virtual assistant has helped drive £2 million in sales, *Digiday UK*, https://digiday.com/marketing/year-marks-spencers-virtual-assistant-helped-drive-2-5m-sales/ (archived at https://perma.cc/T9QN-U49G)

7   Facebook Business (nd) Fuelling growth through mobile, https://www.facebook.com/business/success/asos (archived at https://perma.cc/B6V5-XPSL)

8   Gupta, S (2019) AI-based market research: 10 ways to boost consumer insight, *DZone*, https://dzone.com/articles/ai-based-market-research-10-ways-to-boost-consumer (archived at https://perma.cc/RHV2-W9RZ)

9   AIThority (2018) Transcosmos develops an AI which auto-judges customer service quality at contact centres, https://www.aithority.com/machine-learning/transcosmos-develops-an-ai-which-auto-judges-customer-service-quality/ (archived at https://perma.cc/79LQ-DW3Z)

10  Coldewey, D (2019) Mona Lisa frown: machine learning brings old paintings and photos to life, *Tech Crunch*, https://techcrunch.com/2019/05/22/mona-lisa-frown-machine-learning-brings-old-paintings-and-photos-to-life/ (archived at https://perma.cc/R4YC-F5QN)

11  Hanson, E (2019) From analog ideas to digital dreams, Philippe Starck designs the future with AI, *Autodesk*, https://www.autodesk.com/redshift/philippe-starck-designs/ (archived at https://perma.cc/7SAV-AJQ6)

12  Grush, L (2018) AI software helped NASA dream up this spider-like interplanetary lander, *The Verge*, https://www.theverge.com/2018/11/13/18091448/nasa-ai-autodesk-jpl-lander-europa-enceladus-artificial-intelligence-generative-design (archived at https://perma.cc/U8H7-LQW8)

13  Marr, B (2019) Amazing examples of digital twin technology in practice, *Forbes*, https://www.forbes.com/sites/bernardmarr/2019/04/23/7-amazing-examples-of-digital-twin-technology-in-practice/#42ee2e5e6443 (archived at https://perma.cc/353R-JU5Q)

14  Dhandre, P (2018) Alibaba introduces AI copywriter, *Packt*, https://hub.packtpub.com/alibaba-introduces-ai-copywriter/ (archived at https://perma.cc/5TT7-9AUN)

15  Marr, B (2019) Artificial intelligence can now write amazing content – what does that mean for humans? *Forbes*, https://www.forbes.com/sites/bernardmarr/2019/03/29/artificial-intelligence-can-now-write-amazing-content-what-does-that-mean-for-humans/#969c03750ab0 (archived at https://perma.cc/VH8U-GEVU)

16  Hollinger, P (2016) Meet the cobots: humans and robots together on the factory floor, *Financial Times*, https://www.ft.com/content/6d5d609e-02e2-11e6-af1d-c47326021344 (archived at https://perma.cc/VX2N-PTPU)

17  Dignan, L (2016) Ford tests collaborative robots in German Ford Fiesta plant, *ZDNet*, https://www.zdnet.com/article/ford-tests-collaborative-robots-in-german-ford-fiesta-plant/ (archived at https://perma.cc/R98J-NGEE)

18  Harris, J (2017) Meet your new cobot: is a machine coming for your job; *The Guardian*; https://www.theguardian.com/money/2017/nov/25/cobot-machine-coming-job-robots-amazon-ocado (archived at https://perma.cc/W9VL-9H96)

19  Moon, M (2018) Robots will build robots in $150 million Chinese factory, *Engadget*, https://www.engadget.com/2018/10/27/abb-robotics-factory-china/ (archived at https://perma.cc/Z28A-884K)

20  Marr, B (2018) Amazing real-world examples of 3D printing in 2018, *Forbes*, https://www.forbes.com/sites/bernardmarr/2018/08/22/7-amazing-real-world-examples-of-3d-printing-in-2018/#5ffa158d6585 (archived at https://perma.cc/Z5AM-YFAS)

21  Bharadwaj, R (2019) Artificial intelligence applications in additive manufacturing (3d Printing), *Emerj*, https://emerj.com/ai-sector-overviews/artificial-intelligence-applications-additive-manufacturing-3d-printing/ (archived at https://perma.cc/8TKC-G9F7)

22  Marr, B (nd) ServiceMax: How the Internet of Things (IoT) and predictive maintenance are redefining the field service industry, https://www.bernardmarr.com/default.asp?contentID=1268 (archived at https://perma.cc/7AQ8-CR74)

23  Marr, B (2018) The amazing ways how Unilever uses artificial intelligence to recruit & train thousands of employees, *Forbes*, https://www.forbes.com/sites/bernardmarr/2018/12/14/the-amazing-ways-how-unilever-uses-artificial-intelligence-to-recruit-train-thousands-of-employees/#7626e376274d (archived at https://perma.cc/G3LU-HWDL)

24  Marr, B (2018) The amazing ways how Unilever uses artificial intelligence to recruit & train thousands of employees, *Forbes*, https://www.forbes.com/sites/bernardmarr/2018/12/14/the-amazing-ways-how-unilever-uses-artificial-intelligence-to-recruit-train-thousands-of-employees/#7626e376274d (archived at https://perma.cc/G3LU-HWDL)

25 HPC Wire (2019) Combining machine learning and supercomputing to ferret out phishing attacks, https://www.hpcwire.com/2019/05/23/combining-machine-learning-and-supercomputing-to-ferret-out-phishing-attacks/ (archived at https://perma.cc/D2HW-BQZT)

26 Marr, B (2018) The amazing ways how Mastercard uses artificial intelligence to stop fraud and reduce false declines, *Forbes*, https://www.forbes.com/sites/bernardmarr/2018/11/30/the-amazing-ways-how-mastercard-uses-artificial-intelligence-to-stop-fraud-and-reduce-false-declines/#391697332165 (archived at https://perma.cc/YXH5-V35M)

27 CB Insights (2018) Massive cargo ships are going autonomous, https://www.cbinsights.com/research/autonomous-shipping-trends/ (archived at https://perma.cc/3UZV-F33N)

28 CB Insights (2018) Massive cargo ships are going autonomous, https://www.cbinsights.com/research/autonomous-shipping-trends/ (archived at https://perma.cc/3UZV-F33N)

29 Vincent, J (2019) Ford's vision for package delivery is a robot that folds up into the back of a self-driving car, *The Verge*, https://www.theverge.com/2019/5/22/18635439/robot-package-delivery-ford-agility-robotics-autonomous-digit (archived at https://perma.cc/Y57Q-T8ZQ)

30 Cision PR Newswire (2018) WatchBox offers augmented reality to help e-commerce customers "try on" watches at home before buying, https://www.prnewswire.com/news-releases/watchbox-offers-augmented-reality-to-help-e-commerce-customers-try-on-watches-at-home-before-buying-300639841.html (archived at https://perma.cc/UL2B-KMJQ)

31 Ecommerce News (2017) German ecommerce company Otto uses AI to reduce returns, https://ecommercenews.eu/german-ecommerce-company-otto-uses-ai-reduce-returns/ (archived at https://perma.cc/FVU9-2JYR)

32 Alexander, A (2018) Computer vision case study: Amazon Go, *Medium*, https://medium.com/arren-alexander/computer-vision-case-study-amazon-go-db2c9450ad18 (archived at https://perma.cc/FE62-MPCM)

33 Peterson, H (2019) Walmart reveals it's tracking checkout theft with AI-powered cameras in 1,000 stores, *Business Insider*, https://www.businessinsider.com/walmart-tracks-theft-with-computer-vision-1000-stores-2019-6?r=US&IR=T (archived at https://perma.cc/8XAD-4VAA)

34 Marr, B (2019) Robot-powered pizza, anyone? How automation is transforming the fast-food industry, *Forbes*, https://www.forbes.com/sites/bernardmarr/2019/04/12/robot-powered-pizza-anyone-how-automation-is-transforming-the-fast-food-industry/#50cf09b7427b (archived at https://perma.cc/82HW-LKJN)

35 Kollewe, J and Davies, R (2019) Robocrop: world's first raspberry-picking robot set to work, *Guardian*, https://www.theguardian.com/technology/2019/may/26/world-first-fruit-picking-robot-set-to-work-artificial-intelligence-farming (archived at https://perma.cc/QQ7K-P79U)

36 Health and Safety Executive (2019) Workplace fatal injuries in Great Britain, 2019, https://www.hse.gov.uk/statistics/pdf/fatalinjuries.pdf (archived at https://perma.cc/HED6-W7R5)

37 Marr, B (2019) The amazing ways artificial intelligence (AI) can now detect dangers at work, *Forbes*, https://www.forbes.com/sites/bernardmarr/2019/06/07/the-amazing-ways-artificial-intelligence-ai-can-now-detect-dangers-at-work/#70cf6b037b49 (archived at https://perma.cc/4VPE-TCFT)

PART THREE

# Getting ready for the intelligence revolution

# CHAPTER SEVEN

# Finding the AI opportunities in your business

So far in this book we've looked at the many ways in which organizations are using AI to drive success. But, as with any aspect of business, what works for one company may not work for yours. This chapter will help you start to develop a robust AI strategy that's designed with your business's needs in mind.

## Forget the technology, AI starts with strategy

AI can mean big changes for a business, and these changes can sometimes be disruptive, expensive and time consuming. Therefore, whether you're implementing new AI-driven processes, redesigning your service offering to be more intelligent, making your products smarter, or whatever, it's vital you know *why* you're making such changes. It's vital you know how these steps will help the business achieve its objectives, grow and prosper. If not, you're in danger of falling into the 'technology for technology's sake' trap. Yes, AI can do some pretty amazing things, but if it's not going to help you drive business success, why bother?

### Avoiding AI for AI's sake

AI is exciting. AI will, in time, revolutionize every business across every industry. AI is here to stay.

All those statements are true. But it's also true that AI can be complicated and expensive to implement, it requires a lot of data to work effectively, and it can take time to deliver return on investment. Therefore, it's important not to get carried away and implement AI here, there and everywhere, just because the technology exists. Just because something can be analysed or automated or augmented through AI, doesn't mean it should be. Not every problem can or should be solved with AI. (After all, you can use a jackhammer to crack a walnut, but a nutcracker achieves the same goal with a lot less hassle, noise and expense. It's the same with AI.)

So, while you shouldn't sit on your hands and ignore the potential of AI, diving in without thinking is just as bad – often worse. You should never rush to adopt AI (or any other technology, for that matter) without a clear business need or goal in mind. Ultimately, it's about looking at what your business is trying to achieve, and what unique challenges your business is facing, and then finding potential solutions through AI.

This is where your overarching business strategy comes in. Linking your AI strategy to your business strategy is the best way to ensure AI delivers maximum value for the business. Your AI strategy should be geared around finding intelligent ways to deliver your company's strategic goals, answer your most pressing business questions, and overcome your biggest business challenges. In other words, AI should be used to turn your company strategy into reality. If a potential use of AI doesn't link to your business strategy, alarm bells should be going off. Big, loud alarm bells. Because you're in danger of getting swept up in AI for AI's sake. If you can't see how a particular use of AI will help you achieve your strategic goals, then it's unlikely to be worth the expense and disruption.

### Making sure your business strategy is still relevant

The best use of AI is linked to your strategic organizational goals, that much is clear. Yet, too many businesses try to apply AI to an outdated business strategy or irrelevant business model. For example, they may try to automate business processes that no longer fit with changing customer requirements, or they may introduce AI to a product that's fast becoming obsolete. So, before you start developing your AI strategy, take some time to review your overarching business strategy. Ask yourself, 'Is our business strategy still relevant in this intelligence revolution?' If the answer is no, you need to update your business strategy before you even think about developing an AI strategy. Keep in mind that, for many companies, the intelligence revolution is bringing about huge transformations in their underlying business model – such as Apple transitioning from a product company to more of a smart service provider. (Read examples of how other companies have transformed their business models later in the chapter.)

And if you're confident your business strategy is still current and relevant, then you can start to identify the ways in which AI can help you deliver that strategy. These are your AI opportunities or use cases. More on that coming up after a quick case study.

### AI opportunities at Shell

Royal Dutch Shell is one company I've worked with to help define their AI and data approach. Shell is a business that's not necessarily challenged by lots of tech startups moving into their field (unlike, say, the financial industry, as we saw in Chapter 5). However, as a company, Shell recognizes the importance of using AI to deliver its core strategic objectives of:[1]

- thriving in the energy transition;
- providing a world-class investment case;
- sustaining a strong societal licence to operate.

Let's take the first strategic ambition as an example – to thrive in the energy transition. The energy market is undergoing some dramatic changes right now, and Shell sees AI as being central to overcoming business challenges related to this transition. Encouraging motorists to switch to electric vehicles is a key part of reducing $CO_2$ emissions, but it involves a bit of a chicken-and-egg problem; motorists are reluctant to make the switch to electric vehicles because of the lack of charging terminals, and forecourt operators are slow to adopt electric charging terminals because of lack of demand.

To help overcome supply and demand issues, Shell has rolled out AI at its public electric car charging stations to help monitor, predict and manage demand for charging terminals throughout the day. For example, if more motorists charge up on their way to work, that creates a heavy load on the grid early in the morning – which, crucially, can't be filled by solar power because it's too early in the day. By understanding customers' usage, Shell can better predict loads, and potentially change customer energy consumption patterns to take advantage of renewable energy (for example, by encouraging more people to charge up at lunchtime, when there's more solar power on the grid). This means more energy can be fulfilled by solar, helping to meet Shell's ambition of thriving in the energy transition – and helping to reduce costs for consumers, which should encourage increased demand for electric vehicles. The programme, called RechargePlus, has so far been rolled out in California.[2]

Shell's commitment to using AI to deliver its goals is so impressive, it's even drawn praise from the tech sector. Speaking at the Ignite Conference in 2018, Microsoft CEO Satya Nadella described Shell's use of AI as 'pretty amazing', saying 'they've got a very deliberate strategy of using AI across their entire operation'.[3] And Tom Siebel, CEO of AI software company C3 IoT, has said Shell has 'the largest AI deployment that we are aware of anywhere in the world. Everybody else is kind of looking at it. These guys are rolling it out.'[4]

## Pinpointing the AI opportunities in your business

Getting the best out of AI means identifying the biggest opportunities for *your* business. How can AI help your business deliver its strategic goals? How can AI help your business overcome its biggest challenges? Having reviewed your business strategy, as discussed earlier in the chapter, you're now ready to begin the process of creating a relevant AI strategy. For me, this starts with:

1 Identifying the potential applications (use cases) of AI in your business.
2 Whittling those potential use cases down to just a few (one to three) top-priority use cases, coupled with one or two 'quick-win' AI uses – more on what I mean by quick wins coming up later.

### Step 1. Identifying your use cases

In this first phase, don't limit yourself to a small number of potential AI projects or use cases – you'll be cutting down your use cases to a more manageable number in the next phase. For now, think more about your overall business strategy and consider how AI could help your organization achieve those goals. You can always enlist an AI consultant to help with this process.

Because your AI use cases will be driven by your business strategy, every company will have its own unique set of use cases. An AI priority for one company may not be relevant to another. However, as we saw in Part Two, some general ways organizations use AI are as follows (several of these may apply to your business, and you may have other uses that are more specific to your industry, business challenges, etc):

- making your products more intelligent;
- developing more intelligent services;
- building a deeper understanding of customers;
- making business processes more intelligent;
- automating core business functions;
- automating time-consuming, repetitive or mundane tasks.

Having pinpointed some potential uses in your business, you can now begin to flesh them out in more detail. To do this, I recommend you use the accompanying AI Use Case Template found in the Appendix.

Within the template, you'll see there are 10 sections to complete, and these sections are designed to help you define each use case in more detail. The idea is you fill in a separate template for each of your use cases.

So, working through the template in order, for each use case, you'll need to consider:

1  **Link to strategic goal.** First up, it's vital you can link your use case to a strategic business goal. How would this use of AI help the business achieve its objectives, grow and prosper? In other words, why bother going to all this trouble in the first place? Avoid AI for AI's sake.

2  **AI objective.** Here, you can define your AI-related goal in more detail. What, specifically, are you hoping to achieve through this use of AI? For example, you may be looking to solve a particular business-critical problem, answer key business questions, boost revenue, reduce employee turnover, improve health and safety, etc.

3  **Measures of success (KPIs).** This section answers the question, 'What does success look like for this AI project, and how will we measure success?' Be as specific as you can, and identify which business metrics/KPIs you'll use to track progress against your AI objective.

4 **Use case owner.** In my experience, if you don't make someone accountable for a project, it never gets done. So who in the business would be responsible for this AI use case? Sure, that use case owner would probably need to enlist the help of others (perhaps from inside and outside the business), but the important thing is that one person has overall ownership of the project.

5 **AI approach and data required.** As we saw in Chapter 2, AI encompasses a number of subdivisions (such as machine learning, deep learning, computer vision, etc) and touches on many other technology trends (such as IoT devices, blockchain, etc). Which approach is required to achieve your AI objective, and what sort of data do you need? You can read more about this in Chapter 10.

6 **Ethical and legal issues.** Turn to Chapter 9 to read more about the need for ethics and transparency in AI – it's a huge topic right now. You'll need to consider the potential legal implications of your AI use case (including consent and data privacy), as well as the ethical implications. In other words, how can you ensure your use of AI makes a positive contribution to the business, its employees and its customers?

7 **Technology and infrastructure.** It's very likely each use case will require some technology and infrastructure changes. Here, you consider what systems, software and hardware you might need to achieve your AI objective. Read more about technology and infrastructure in Chapter 11.

8 **Skills and capacity.** AI also brings with it certain challenges around skills, capabilities, capacity and resourcing, especially for smaller and mid-sized companies. Consider the skills gaps that might prevent you from achieving your AI objective – and how will you close those gaps? This may involve training staff, hiring new talent or partnering with external providers. Read more about the people and skills side of AI in Chapter 8.

9 **Implementation.** This is where you set out the potential implementation challenges and roadblocks that you'll need to overcome if your AI objective is to become reality. This will likely involve some leadership challenges, which I talk more about in Chapter 12.

10 **Change management.** This is normally lumped in with implementation, but I tend to separate it out to emphasize how vital it is

to manage AI-related changes carefully – after all, AI may lead to big changes in how your business operates. For example, if you're automating or streamlining processes, this may impact the work of your employees, so how will you manage this while promoting a positive AI culture? I touch more on this in the people and culture chapter (Chapter 8).

Repeat this process and complete the same template for each of the AI use cases that you've identified. This process will help you evaluate and prioritize your use cases in order of strategic importance, which brings me to…

## Step 2. Working out your AI priorities

Depending on your business, you may have identified as many as 10 or 15 use cases in the previous phase. Trying to embark on too many AI projects at once can spell disaster, so you now need to rank your use cases in order of their strategic importance to the business. What you want to end up with is:

- **Your top one, two or three key strategic use cases.** These are your absolute top AI priorities for now – the AI use cases that represent the biggest opportunities for your business, or will help solve your biggest business challenges. If you're a smaller business, you may only want to focus on one key AI priority at a time. For a bigger business, two or three should be doable. But don't be tempted to prioritize more than three key AI use cases – sticking to a smaller number ensures your AI strategy remains focused and achievable.
- **One or two AI 'quick wins'.** I've found it really helps to identify one or two short-term, smaller AI projects that are relatively quick, easy and inexpensive. Your key AI priorities may take some time to implement, so identifying a couple of quick wins allows you to demonstrate the value of AI, help to win people over, and sow the seeds for a culture of AI.

Having identified your AI priorities, you can then start to identify the common themes, issues and requirements across those use cases. I have a template for this, too – see the AI Strategy Template ('AI Strategy on a Page') in the Appendix. This template forms the basis of your formal AI strategy.

Looking at the template, you'll see there's space to include your one, two or three most pressing AI priorities at the top, plus your one or two quick wins. The rest of the template is broken down into requirements like technology and skills (which will be familiar to you from the AI Use Case Template, from the previous step). In each of these sections, your task is to pinpoint the challenges, themes, activities, issues and goals that are common across your top-priority and quick-win use cases. We do this because, even though each use case/AI project is different, they're bound to share some common issues or challenges – such as getting access to the right data. By identifying these shared themes early on, you can find the most efficient, effective ways to overcome them.

So, in order of the template, identify your:

- **Common data strategy issues.** AI doesn't work without data, so you may need to revisit your data strategy at this point. Read more about data in Chapter 10.
- **Common ethical and legal issues.** Turn to Chapter 9 for more on this.
- **Common technology and infrastructure issues,** as per Chapter 11.
- **Common skills and capacity issues.** These people-related issues are covered in Chapter 8.
- **Common implementation issues.** Common leadership challenges are explored in Chapter 12.
- **Common change management issues,** which is both a leadership challenge (Chapter 12) and a people/skills consideration (Chapter 8).

Completing this template will help you pin down the cross-cutting themes, issues and challenges across your AI priorities – plus, it'll act as a handy, one-page reminder of what you're trying to achieve through AI. Depending on the complexities of your AI priorities, you may also need to develop a more detailed, narrative strategy document that outlines each of the above considerations at greater length.

And as for those use cases that don't make the cut and aren't deemed high priority for now, don't discard them completely. As you achieve one AI project, you may find you have capacity to move onto another use case – or it may be that your overall strategic priorities shift, which means AI use cases that were identified some time ago are no longer relevant. I therefore recommend you repeat this process of identifying and prioritizing use cases at least once a year, or every time you review your overarching business strategy.

## Learning from other businesses that have been on this AI journey

Here, I want to highlight how some other companies have successfully implemented AI in order to overcome their business challenges and deliver their strategic priorities.

### The traditional business

I referenced Shell earlier in the chapter, but let's revisit the example briefly to see how Shell came up with its AI use cases. Shell started by reviewing its overall organizational strategy to make sure those strategic ambitions were still relevant. Then we ran a series of workshops across the business – not just with IT people, but across various business units – to explore potential opportunities for AI. Then, in the process set out previously, we defined these opportunities in more detail and prioritized the use cases according to the company's most pressing business needs. Even though Shell is a large organization with impressive resources, we still limited ourselves to no more than three strategic AI priorities, plus a couple of quick wins – because even large companies (some would say *especially* large companies) run the risk of getting caught up the excitement of AI and losing sight of what they're trying to achieve.

Shell operates in a long-established industry (albeit one that's undergoing massive changes) and has been around for more than a century. How have newer businesses – companies with a strong tech focus from the start – coped with the intelligence revolution?

### The tech trailblazers

Amazon and Alibaba are now both considered leaders in the Big Data and AI-as-a-service field. But it's important to remember that they didn't start out as what I'd call 'AI-native' businesses. With their beginnings in ecommerce (Amazon as an online book retailer, Alibaba as a general online retailer), both were obviously tech-focused from the off. But neither was built with AI at its core – for both Amazon and Alibaba, the AI came later. And, boy, did they take to AI like ducks to water.

Today, Amazon and Alibaba have placed AI at the very core of everything they do: smarter products (such as Alexa and Echo, as per Chapter 4), smarter services (for example, Amazon's personalized customer recommendations, as mentioned in Chapter 5) and smarter business operations (like Alibaba's AI-driven copywriting tool from Chapter 6).

Alibaba is the world's largest ecommerce marketplace, with more global sales than Amazon and eBay combined.[5] It uses AI to boost online sales and manage customer queries – for example, its AI-powered chatbot, Dian Xiaomi, serves more than 3.5 million customers a day, successfully understanding more than 90 per cent of queries.[6] Alibaba also uses robots to fulfil orders in automated warehouses that can process 1 million shipments a day.[7] And it's even turning physical shops into smart stores; under its Tmall brand, Alibaba has overhauled around 1 million mom-and-pop shops and 100 superstores, adding AI-powered apps and technology such as heat sensors that track foot traffic.[8]

Likewise, Amazon has put AI at the centre of everything it does. AI powers Alexa's ability to understand and respond to user requests. It powers the online shopping experience – from search results to predicting what customers want to buy. And through Amazon Web Services, the company's cloud computing subsidiary, Amazon is making AI accessible to companies that otherwise wouldn't have the technology, skills and capacity to deploy it.

These examples show how even extremely tech-savvy businesses have had to reorganize themselves around AI. What really impresses me about Amazon and Alibaba is how seamlessly different divisions across these companies have got behind AI. Building a 'culture of AI' is crucial to deploying AI successfully, and both Amazon and Alibaba demonstrate how such a culture can fuel success right across the business.

## The AI-native business

ByteDance, the company behind the TikTok and Toutiao apps (see Chapter 5), is the world's most valuable startup.[9] Unlike Amazon and Alibaba, ByteDance started as an AI company – all of ByteDance's products, such as TikTok and Toutiao, use AI to deliver the content that users most want to see. ByteDance's systems use AI technologies like computer vision, natural language processing and machine learning (see Chapter 2) to understand and analyse written content, images and videos. Then, based on what the systems know about each user, they can deliver the content they believe each user wants. The more a user interacts with the app (reading articles, watching videos, commenting, etc), the more the machine learning algorithms understand the user's preferences and interests.

The key lesson here is that ByteDance isn't a company that's built AI into its products and services; for ByteDance, AI *is* the product and service.

## Transitioning to an AI business – will it change your entire business model?

Most companies will never reach the AI heights of companies like ByteDance, Amazon and Alibaba, nor do they need to tackle AI on such a huge scale. But what's interesting is many companies are starting to see themselves as AI businesses. Apple is one example that I've already mentioned – transitioning from a computer manufacturer to a company that produces smart products and, increasingly, smart services.

But even outside of the tech world, AI, big data and the intelligence revolution are beginning to impact the very business models on which organizations operate. Let's look at a couple of examples.

### Wimbledon: How the All England Lawn Tennis Club (AELTC) has transitioned to a data-driven media organization

In Chapter 5 I briefly mentioned how IBM's AI Watson tool is being used to create automated highlights of tennis matches. I absolutely love Wimbledon, so let me expand on that example a little. In 2019, I was lucky enough to get a behind-the-scenes glimpse of how the AELTC and IBM are using AI to deliver a great user experience.

In 2018, the AELTC took over broadcasting the Wimbledon tournament from the BBC, meaning TV cameras and broadcast output are now controlled in-house via an operation called Wimbledon Broadcasting Services.[10] This was part of a deliberate move to transition the AELTC from a tennis club to a data-driven media organization – one that's capable of creating and tailoring content for a global audience, and (through Wimbledon's partnership with IBM's AI technology) delivering an exciting digital experience for viewers.

In one example, Wimbledon now offers an online and app-based AR experience that lets fans see what's happening on the practice courts – an area that's normally off-limits to the public. And, as I mentioned in Chapter 5, fans can now watch AI-generated daily highlights that are curated by IBM Watson using video analytics and sound analytics (essentially, pinpointing the most exciting parts of the day's matches based on factors like player gestures and crowd reactions). Using AI, this process of creating highlights packages from hundreds of hours of footage can now be completed within two minutes of a match finishing.[11] What's more, IBM has introduced a new tool, called OpenScale, to ensure there's no bias in how the highlights are generated – for example, if certain matches have a smaller crowd size, the AI can factor this into the process of ranking highlights to ensure highlights are generated in a fair, balanced way – and that no exciting moments get missed.

With technology like this behind the tournament, the AELTC is fast transitioning to an AI-powered media organization that has full control over its own output.

### Banking in the app age: how one bank now sees itself as a software company

In Chapter 5, I mentioned how many traditional banks have struggled to pre-empt and combat the fintech startups that are moving into their territory and offering cooler, more competitive products. Many long-standing banks face significant challenges in adopting AI, such as:

- clunky legacy IT systems;
- a culture that may not place much emphasis on AI;
- a mindset where banking is seen almost as a utility, something that everyone needs – which, to put it bluntly, leads some banks to ignore the need to add real value for their customers.

As a result, many fintech startups have been able to move into traditional banking territory and woo customers with value-added services. For example, Pleo offers a business credit card with an accompanying app that automatically manages your expenses. Users can either take a picture of their receipt, or if a receipt has been sent via email, the app will recognize this and upload the details itself. The transaction is then automatically categorized into the correct expense format (for example, whether spending at a petrol station was on food or fuel) – meaning users no longer have to spend precious time completing expense reports. A new wave of financial apps have been challenging traditional current and savings accounts, helping people save and manage their money in a way that many traditional banks don't. For example, app-based bank

Monzo offers customers a full current account service, but with value-added services like letting customers round up transactions to the nearest pound, with the difference going into a separate savings pot.

But some traditional banks are fighting back against these cheeky upstarts. Take BBVA, Spain's second-largest bank, with a history that dates back to 1857, as an example. BBVA has put AI at the centre of its transformation strategy – and as far back as 2015, the then company executive chairman was claiming 'BBVA will be a software company in the future'.[12] Creating a customer-centric platform was one of its first priorities in this respect, including a suite of mobile banking apps. This includes the Bconomy app (created in collaboration with Google Cloud), which helps customers manage their money by predicting future income and expenses for the next month. BBVA's Valora app gives homebuyers price information on houses for sales, and comparable sales figures for similar homes that sold nearby. The company also has an AI-based, in-app digital voice assistant called MIA that allows customers to complete transactions using voice commands. BBVA has also been spending some serious money on fintech mergers and acquisitions – investments estimated at around $1 billion – and is now the largest shareholder of digital-only bank Atom.[13] All this momentum is starting to pay off – a 2018 report by Forrester Research named BBVA top of global mobile banking apps[14] – and it certainly moves the company closer to its goal of becoming a software company, not just a straightforward banking provider.

---

**KEY TAKEAWAYS**

In this chapter we've learned:

- Successful AI starts with strategy, not the technology itself. Your AI strategy should be linked to your overarching business strategy – meaning AI should help you achieve your organizational objectives. But first, make sure your overarching business strategy is current and appropriate for the intelligence revolution. Don't apply AI to an outdated business strategy.

- Creating your AI strategy starts with two steps (both aided by the templates in Chapter 14):

  - Identifying potential applications (use cases) of AI in your business.

-     ○ Prioritizing these use cases in order of strategic importance. You want to end up with the top one, two or three strategic use cases, plus a couple of quick wins that can be implemented quickly to demonstrate the value of AI.
- Repeat this process of identifying and prioritizing your AI use cases at least every year or every time you review your business strategy.
- From long-standing companies to tech startups and AI natives, AI is increasingly becoming central to organizations. For many, AI, big data and the intelligence revolution is bringing about a transformation in the organization's business model.

Identifying and prioritizing your AI uses is one thing; turning them into reality is quite another. For any organization to successfully implement AI, it's vital to build a culture that embraces AI – despite the many changes it may bring to the organization. In the next chapter, I explore what AI may mean for the people who work in your business, and how to get your people on board with the intelligence revolution.

## Endnotes

1   Shell, Our strategy, https://www.shell.com/investors/shell-and-our-strategy/our-strategy.html (archived at https://perma.cc/8RXL-Q73V)

2   Shell, Shell RechargePlus: Managed smart charging for electric vehicles, https://www.shell.us/business-customers/shellrechargeplus.html (archived at https://perma.cc/GC8N-BK2C)

3   Konathala, S (2018) Text of Satya Nadella's keynote speech at Ignite Conference 2018, *Medium*, https://medium.com/techinpieces/text-of-satya-nadellas-keynote-speech-at-ignite-conference-2018-4141077384f6 (archived at https://perma.cc/4MG4-53YK)

4   Financial Times, The week in energy: AI and oil, https://www.ft.com/content/d67962d8-c0d8-11e8-95b1-d36dfef1b89a (archived at https://perma.cc/59R6-K3E6)

5   Cheng, A (2017) Alibaba vs The World, *Institutional Investor*, https://www.institutionalinvestor.com/article/b1505pjf8xsy75/alibaba-vs-the-world (archived at https://perma.cc/8C5V-KWSZ)

6   Chec, C and Dai, S (7017) Alibaba lets AI, robots and drones do the heavy lifting on Singles' Day, *South China Morning Post*, https://www.scmp.com/tech/innovation/article/2119359/alibaba-lets-ai-robots-and-drones-do-heavy-lifting-singles-day (archived at https://perma.cc/7JMF-H7W3)

7   Marr, B (1028) The amazing ways Chinese tech giant Alibaba uses artificial intelligence and machine learning, *Forbes*, https://www.forbes.com/sites/bernardmarr/2018/07/23/

the-amazing-ways-chinese-tech-giant-alibaba-uses-artificial-intelligence-and-machine-learning/#736a9b63117a (archived at https://perma.cc/LWR2-AJPX)

8   Levine, S (2017) China's AI-infused corner store of the future, *Axios*, https://www.axios.com/china-alibaba-tencent-jd-com-artificial-intelligence-corner-store-df90517e-befb-40ca-82d5-f37caa738d54.html (archived at https://perma.cc/3KW2-HAL7)

9   Byford, S (2018) How China's ByteDance became the world's most valuable startup, *The Verge*, https://www.theverge.com/2018/11/30/18107732/bytedance-valuation-tiktok-china-startup (archived at https://perma.cc/ZMT2-YBD9)

10  Nelson, A (2017) Wimbledon to launch in-house host broadcaster, *SportsPro*, https://www.sportspromedia.com/news/wimbledon-to-launch-in-house-host-broadcaster (archived at https://perma.cc/VQ2G-WQNR)

11  IBM (2019) First serve: Wimbledon daily video highlights curated by IBM Watson, the AI behind The Championships, *Telegraph*, https://www.telegraph.co.uk/tennis/artificial-intelligence/wimbledon-daily-video-highlights/ (archived at https://perma.cc/VE22-T9KV)

12  Marr, B (2019) BBVA, Spain's second-largest bank, is using artificial intelligence to transform itself, https://www.linkedin.com/pulse/bbva-spains-second-largest-bank-using-artificial-transform-marr/ (archived at https://perma.cc/GH36-AEN6)

13  Grynkiewicz, T (2018) A billion dollar bet on the future: Fintech Investment Leader BBVA just showed how to deal with Amazon and Google, https://www.netguru.com/blog/fintech-investment-bbva-amazon-and-google (archived at https://perma.cc/A7DW-ZSNY)

14  Forrester Research (2018) The Forrester banking wave: global mobile apps summary, https://www.forrester.com/report/The+Forrester+Banking+Wave+Global+Mobile+Apps+Summary+2018/-/E-RES144696 (archived at https://perma.cc/354R-XXRT)

# CHAPTER EIGHT

# Addressing people and culture needs

You cannot become an intelligent organization without the right people and culture. No business will ever succeed with AI if it hasn't got the right skills and capabilities, or if the entire company isn't on board with AI and data initiatives. That's why I believe this chapter to be one of the most important in this book.

To start this chapter, I'll explore how advances in AI will transform the way we work. Naturally, as the world of work changes, a different set of skills and capabilities will become more critical for success – both at an individual level and an organizational level. We're not just talking about technical skills and capabilities (although they are obviously important), but soft skills, too – things like the ability to cope with change, or the ability to think creatively in order to solve problems and find innovative solutions.

And as organizations evolve, it's really important to think carefully about how to take everyone, at every level of the company, on this journey. Change makes people nervous after all, so organizations will have to work hard to manage change, overcome fear and build a positive AI culture – a culture that embraces AI and data as key ingredients for success. A culture that sees AI as an opportunity to make work better for all of us, rather than something to fear.

Finally, this chapter is written not just with the organization's needs in mind, but your needs as an individual. In other words, I hope this chapter will prompt you to think about your own skills and capabilities, and the areas in which you might need to learn and develop in order to add value to your organization, and to futureproof your own career.

## How the world of work will change

Technology has always brought about new ways of working – think of the impact computers and digital technology (the third industrial revolution) have had on how we work. But the intelligence revolution, this fourth industrial revolution, feels unprecedented in terms of the sheer pace of change. There's no doubt that AI is going to fundamentally change the work that humans do (and, as we'll see in this section, potentially change the way we think about work). But we're not talking about generational changes here. We're not talking about how, in the future, your children and grandchildren will do entirely new jobs (although they will); we're talking about enormous transformations that are going to take place within the next five, 10 or 20 years – in your working lifetime. You as an individual, and your organization, must start to prepare for these changes. Because, believe me, they're coming.

### The future impact of automation

Increasing automation is an obvious place to start since a common theme of AI is 'be afraid: robots are going to take all our jobs'. I don't want to downplay it – in many industries and jobs, the impact of automation will be keenly felt; but I do want to paint a more positive picture than the usual 'all workers are doomed' spin.

Let's start with the stark figures, though. To understand the impact of automation, PricewaterhouseCoopers analysed more than 200,000 jobs in 29 countries and found:[1]

- By the early 2020s, 3 per cent of jobs will be at risk of automation.
- That rises to almost 20 per cent by the late 2020s.
- By the mid-2030s, 30 per cent of jobs will be at potential risk of automation. For workers with low education, this rises to 44 per cent.
- No sector will be unaffected by these changes but some industries will be impacted more than others.

- AI, robotics and automation could provide a potential $15 trillion boost to global GDP by 2030.

That last point provides some crucial balance. While automation will no doubt displace many existing jobs, PwC predicts it will also generate demand for many new jobs. In other words, it'll create new jobs and new opportunities. I tend to agree. Just as the previous industrial revolutions have ultimately created more jobs, and better jobs, the intelligence revolution will create more jobs than it destroys – and, importantly, my hope is it'll create *better* jobs for humans.

In fact, AI has been described as 'the greatest job engine the world has ever seen'.[2] Rather like the internet before it. Yes, the internet had a negative impact on some jobs (for example, how many of us now book flights and hotels online, instead of popping to our local travel agent?), but look how many jobs it's created and how it's enabled businesses to branch into new markets, reach new customers, streamline their business processes…

So why are we so concerned about AI and automation? Partly it's because we can't imagine what the jobs of the future will be. Think back to the year 2000 and some of the careers that didn't exist before Y2K:

- Data scientist
- Drone pilot
- Social media influencer
- Social media manager
- Vlogger
- App developer
- Data compliance officer

Imagine yourself in the year 2000, trying to tell a careers adviser you want to be a social media influencer or app designer! They'd have no clue what you were talking about. It's the same with the jobs of 2040; we can't yet imagine what they are, but they're coming.

(As an example, one 2019 news story about a digital dress that sold for almost $10,000 gives us a glimpse of a potential new industry.[3] The dress doesn't exist in real life, and can only be seen online, but it can be tailored to you based on a photo. Someone bought it for $9,500. Does this mean 'digital fashion designer' will be a sought-after career in the future? Perhaps.)

So, the concern over AI and automation is partly due to our inability to envision the work of the future. It's also partly due to the fact that some of the figures on automation are sometimes misrepresented. Saying that a large percentage of jobs are at potential risk of automation doesn't necessarily mean that all those jobs will disappear and be replaced by robots. In some cases, it may mean that *parts* of the job may be automated or augmented through AI, which may then change the nature of that job. Let's take radiologists as an example. Just because computers can now read and analyse patient scans doesn't mean we'll no longer need radiologists. But it likely means the work of radiologists will change. Instead of spending many hours a day reviewing scans, they might spend just a portion reviewing patient scans – those cases where the computer has flagged a potential abnormality that needs closer attention – allowing more time for patient care, treatment strategies, and so on.

Research by Capgemini backs up this idea of AI augmenting rather than displacing human workers altogether. In a survey of 1,000 organizations that have already deployed AI-based systems, four out of five had *created* more jobs.[4] To find out more, I spoke to one of the survey respondents, insurance giant Prudential. The company's global head of AI, Michael Natusch told me, 'Instead of looking for ways to replace humans with AI, we are seeking the most fruitful complements.'[5] He cites robotic call centre assistants as one example. 'Clearly, nobody wants to talk to a robot. But if a robot answers a phone call on the second ring and provides the right information at the right moment in time, then there is value in this. Our call centre agents appreciate the collaboration with robots as they are now able to focus on harder problems that require their experience, creativity and empathy.'

This brings us to a key point. If we're honest with ourselves, the tasks that are most likely to be automated by AI are not the tasks best suited to humans – or the tasks that humans should even *want* to do. Machines are great at automating the boring, mundane and repetitive stuff, those tasks that are easily repeatable, rules-based and uncreative. In the age of AI, are those tasks really the best use of a human worker's time, when we know that humans excel at more creative, empathetic and interpersonal work? Think of our example radiologist – do they really want to spend all day in a room looking at images from CT scans? Or would they rather spend more time on patient care?

It's early days, of course, but the signs are encouraging. Organizations currently making use of AI applications are generally finding it augments the existing human workforce, rather than making it redundant. To put it another way, AI is helping people do their jobs more efficiently and add greater value to the organization.

## A new working experience for employees

AI is already changing so many aspects of how we live our lives, it makes sense that it'll also change our working lives. The employee experience of the future will change dramatically, even in seemingly non-tech companies – that's if there's even such a thing as a non-tech company in the future, as every company comes to rely more and more on technology.

For one thing, physical robots and cobots (see Chapter 6) will have an increasing presence in many workplaces; we have seen this already in manufacturing and warehousing environments. But even in office environments, workers will have to get used to AI tools as 'co-workers'. From how people are recruited, to how they learn and develop in the job, to their everyday working activities, AI technology and smart machines will play an increasingly prominent role in the average person's working life. Just as we've all got used to tools like email and messaging apps, we'll also get used to routinely using tools that monitor workflows and processes, and make intelligent suggestions about how things could be done more efficiently or effectively. Tools will carry out more and more repetitive admin tasks such as arranging meetings and managing a diary. And, very likely, tools will monitor how employees are working and flag up when someone is having trouble with a task or not following procedures correctly (for example, safety rules).

This means we're likely to see much more monitoring of employee activity and performance – which some would call 'employee surveillance'. It's already happening. A survey by Gartner found that more than 50 per cent of companies with a turnover above $750 million are using digital data-gathering tools to monitor employee activities and performance.[6] As an example of this sort of monitoring, workplace analytics specialists Humanyze can analyse staff emails and messaging data, along with data from name badges equipped with microphones, to better understand employee interactions.[7] The use of tools like these naturally makes some people distinctly uncomfortable, and makes the topic of ethics, trust and transparency all the more important (see Chapter 9).

All this means the future of work for employees will be very different to how it is today, and the changes will come thick and fast. On top of this, the workforce itself is changing in several key ways. For example:

- **Workforces are becoming decentralized.** For many jobs, employees no longer need to be in the same location, meaning the next generation of workers can choose to live anywhere, rather than going where the work is.
- **Positions are becoming more fluid.** The gig economy will continue to expand, but also within organizations, positions will be more fluid. People will have multiple roles in one place of employment.
- **Employees are becoming lifelong learners.** The lifespan for skillsets is shrinking, and technology will continue to evolve, meaning everyone will be required to adapt their skills throughout their working lives.

### The rise of the 'superjob'

I've already alluded to how, when parts of jobs are automated by machines, that frees up humans for work that is generally more creative and people-oriented, requiring skills such as problem solving, empathy, listening, communication, interpretation, and collaboration – all skills that humans are still better at than machines. In other words, the jobs of the future will focus more and more on the human element and soft skills.

Importantly, these skills aren't fixed tasks like the work involved in many traditional jobs, and this may lead to less rigidly defined job roles in the future. In its 2019 Global Human Capital Trends survey, Deloitte explored the impact of AI on jobs. According to Deloitte, as machines take on the mundane, repetitive work, jobs become more human, which makes the work and contribution of people in the workplace more valuable and important. This is borne out by the 2019 survey results:[8]

- 62 per cent of respondents are using automation to eliminate transactional work and replace repetitive tasks;
- 47 per cent are using automation to improve existing work practices and boost productivity;
- 36 per cent are 'redesigning work' as a result of automation.

What does this 'redesigning' mean in practice? As people find themselves working across different job roles, teams and projects, organizational structures may become more flexible and fluid as a result. According to Deloitte, this creates new categories of work:

- **Standard jobs:** Generally focusing on repeatable tasks and standardized processes, standard jobs use a specified and narrow skill set.
- **Hybrid jobs:** These roles require a combination of technical and soft skills – which traditionally haven't been combined in the same job.
- **Superjobs:** These are roles that combine work and responsibilities from multiple traditional jobs, where technology is used to both augment and widen the scope of the work, involving a more complex combination of technical and human skills.

From Gartner's analysis, it's clear that employees and organizations will need to develop both the technical and softer human skills to succeed in the age of AI. I talk more about both technical and soft skills for success later in the chapter.

### Bracing for the challenges – and opportunities

This new world of work will bring with it some challenges, and not everyone will be ready or adapt smoothly to the changes that are coming our way. While I'm optimistic about the overall impact AI will have on jobs, the economy, and the work that humans do, it won't all be good. Some people will lose their jobs, and some of the new jobs being created won't be high-quality, rewarding, creative work. We won't all be doing 'superjobs' in 2035.

As one example of this, advances in AI and big data have given rise to microtasks and 'ghost workers'.[9] To put it bluntly, this is where people are paid peanuts to do the mundane, repetitive tasks that power the AI economy, such as tidying up datasets for huge tech giants, or identifying objects in images. It's a largely unknown army of generally poorly paid workers that make advances in AI technology possible.

However, in the main, AI presents many exciting opportunities to enhance the work of humans. But making the most of this will require organizations – and the people who work for them – to develop both the technical and soft skills necessary to cope with the changing nature of work. It will also require something of a cultural shift for organizations – more on that coming up later in the chapter. For now, let's explore the skills that are necessary for success in the intelligence revolution, starting with technical skills.

## Building the right technical skills

When I talk to people about AI, big data and the intelligence revolution, they often want to know what skills we should develop (both at an individual and an organizational level) to prepare ourselves for the transformations coming our way. Technical skills are a key area in which we all need to develop – and this may range from the more complex end of the scale, with things like data science, to the less complex, such as becoming more technology-literate.

The level of knowledge and skills required by the organization and you as an individual will depend on your industry and role. However, I believe that absolutely everyone will need to develop a certain level of comfort around technology. There's no getting away from the fact that the fourth industrial revolution is fuelled by technological innovations, including AI, big data, blockchains, virtual reality, and so on. Employees at most levels will be required to access data and work out what action to take based on what the data tells them. And everyone must be able to understand the potential impact of new technologies on their industry, company, and job.

### Avoiding automation bias

In business, assumptions can be dangerous things. The beauty of Big Data and AI is that it gives people the tools to make decisions based on hard data, rather than their assumptions, biases and gut feelings. But it's not all rosy. In fact, the rapid advance of AI and automation may enable a potentially very troublesome bias for businesses: automation bias.

What exactly is automation bias? Ever read a story of someone blindly following their sat nav and driving into the sea or half-way up a mountain and getting stuck? (In fact, while I was writing this book, a comedian on the radio was describing how he and his partner were driving to the South of France. When the sat nav started directing them north, the comedian pointed out that it might be wrong, since the South of France was clearly not north. But in the driver's seat, his partner carried on regardless. They ended up in Belgium – many hundreds of kilometres from the South of France.)

Someone following their sat nav to the letter even though it's pretty obviously leading them astray is just one example of automation bias – the human tendency to trust and depend on automated systems over and above our own judgment. We outsource decision making to the machine, and just do what it tells us. As a result, we can override correct decisions in favour of incorrect automated information. Like driving to Belgium.

In an increasingly automated world, the danger is that companies and their workers will blindly follow automated systems. But what we need to remember is that AI and automated systems are only as good as the data they're trained with, the data they continued to be fed, and the algorithms they're programmed to follow. If there's a flaw in the data, training or the analysis, the output will be flawed as well. This is why organizations must prioritize key human skills like critical thinking, reasoning and empathy, alongside technical skills, so that they can get the best out of machines and humans working together – rather than humans simply being led by machines. Read more about the essential soft or human skills for success later in the chapter.

Good governance is also essential in the fight against automation bias – so that the data itself isn't biased, or the system programmed with certain biases in mind. Read more about the ethical use of AI in Chapter 9.

The potential for automation bias also means that people at all levels of the organization need to become more data literate – so that we can understand the limitations of technology as well as its potential. So that we know enough to understand why automated systems make the decisions they do. Which brings me to...

### The need to raise data literacy across the organization

Even those who aren't data scientists need to be able to understand technology, specifically AI and data – how it works at a basic level, what it can do, how it supports decision making, and, of course, its limitations. If we raise data literacy, people can become more analytical themselves, rather than blindly follow what AI tells them.

The true objective of data literacy is to give everyone access to the right data so that every business unit can use it to make better decisions that will lead to business success. This isn't just about being able to read numbers and charts; it's about being able to extrapolate useful meaning from the data, think critically about what the data is saying, and then put those insights into action.

At an organizational level, the level of data literacy can be measured as the 'digital IQ' – meaning the organization's ability to harness and profit from technology. According to a 2017 study by PwC, the digital IQs of most companies have dropped, not increased, despite overall increases in the resources devoted to digital.[10] This is perhaps due to the sheer pace of technology advances these days, making it difficult for companies to keep up. But despite the challenges, if companies don't invest in raising their digital IQ, they risk being left behind. This goes for every business, in every industry or sector.

The more data literate your organization is – the more you can raise your digital IQ – the better your results will be. The PwC survey supports this, finding that organizations that embrace policies and practices to improve their digital IQ are the top performers financially. In the 21st century, data literacy will propel momentum and success, just as literacy did in the 20th century.

Having a data-literate workforce means that employees will be able to use data and AI to influence their day-to-day activities and decisions, perform their job better and contribute to overall company performance. It means that everyone will have access to the data they need to perform their job successfully – and, crucially, that they'll have the tools to make sense of that data and don't have to wait for data scientists to interpret it for them. And it means that employees will understand the importance of data, and how to handle it appropriately. This should also have the added advantage of reducing the number of data breaches, since employees are currently responsible for 40 per cent of security breaches.[11]

## How to build data literacy

Despite the challenges involved, raising data literacy in your organization will help you gain a competitive advantage. When I work with a company, I recommend the following steps to promote and boost data literacy:

1 Establish your current data literacy.
2 Identify data advocates.
3 Communicate why data literacy is important.
4 Ensure access to data.
5 Create your data literacy training programme.
6 Start small and continually assess your needs.
7 Lead by example.

Let's explore each step in turn.

ESTABLISHING YOUR CURRENT DATA LITERACY

This may involve asking questions such as, are managers currently able to propose new initiatives backed by relevant data? Or, how many teams are routinely using data to make decisions? Knowing where you are right now gives you an idea of where improvements can be made.

IDENTIFYING DATA ADVOCATES

Pinpoint those individuals who will be strong data leaders and who can help craft a data literacy training programme. These should be people from across different business functions who can champion the benefits of data literacy, determine data literacy gaps, and help to prioritize groups for the data literacy programme. Crucially, they must be able to 'speak' data in a way that's easy for everyone to understand. Data analysts are great at understanding and working with data, but communicating data is another skill altogether. Your data advocates must be able to act as 'translators', bridging the gap between data analysts and business groups, and communicating how to use data to its full potential. Which brings me to…

COMMUNICATING WHY DATA LITERACY IS IMPORTANT

As with any new initiative, when people understand the 'why', they're more likely to support it. Your data advocates will need to explain why data literacy is essential for your organization's success.

ENSURING ACCESS TO DATA

It's vital you have the systems and tools to allow broader access to data, so that people don't have to rely on data experts to be able to manipulate data, extract information and share insights. Self-service tools like management dashboards and data visualization tools are vital for this.

CREATING YOUR DATA LITERACY TRAINING PROGRAMME

As well as training people on the importance of data and how to use the data tools at their disposal, it's vital that teams are taught how to think critically about data if they're to avoid automation bias. Every employee should know to ask questions such as 'How was this data collected?' 'What can be learned from this data?' and 'How reliable is this data?' Employees must also be trained on the safe and ethical handling of data. Remember to make your data literacy training as fun, casual and engaging as possible.

### STARTING SMALL AND CONTINUALLY ASSESSING YOUR NEEDS

Data literacy is an iterative process, not something that can be achieved overnight. So start your training programme with one business unit at a time, not everyone all at once. Prioritize which group needs training the most. What you learn from training one business group can be used to adjust the programme for next time. Be sure to get feedback from groups about what's working and what's not so that your data literacy training becomes more effective over time.

### LEADING BY EXAMPLE

The leaders of your organization need to prioritize data insights in their own work to show how data and AI is critical to decision making and daily operations. In other words, it's 'do as I do', not 'do as I say'. For example, you could insist that any proposals for new products or services are backed up with data and analytics to support those ideas. Over time, this emphasis will help to create a culture of data and AI (more on culture coming up later in the chapter).

As with any new way of working, you'll no doubt encounter barriers to boosting your data literacy. In my experience, some of the biggest barriers tend to be:

- company culture;
- fear;
- data.

Let's look at each area in turn.

### COMPANY CULTURE

There's that word again: culture. Leaders have to practise what they preach if people are going to take data literacy seriously. This approach requires acceptance of change, which can be challenging for people. But resistance to change and the adoption of new skills is often down to a lack of awareness on how data can be used to the company's advantage. When people can see the benefits, they're more likely to support the change. More on culture coming up later in the chapter.

### FEAR

There's no doubt about it, AI and particularly automation makes people nervous. People in the organization might fear being replaced by others who are more tech-savvy. (They might even fear being replaced by a machine.) Or they might fear they'll fail at adopting required new skills. Key to overcoming this is making it clear that the AI revolution doesn't mean everyone has to become data scientists. Data literacy doesn't mean becoming a data scientist. It means understanding the value of data, being able to interpret data, and being able to use data to perform their job better.

### DATA

Yes, the data itself can be a barrier to data literacy. For example, an organization might be collecting a lot of data, but if it's not collecting the right data, or if the data is flawed, then it won't be able to inform decisions as well as it could. Remember, not all data is equally valuable to the organization. If people don't have access to the right data at the right time, it can compromise efforts to boost data literacy.

## Closing the data and AI skills gap in your organization

When it comes to the more advanced data and AI skills, beyond basic data literacy, most organizations are facing a significant skills gap. What I mean by that is most organizations simply haven't got the AI and data skills needed to survive and thrive in the fourth industrial revolution. Therefore, organizations will need to focus on closing the skills gap and building the more advanced technical skills. This can be done by:

- upskilling your existing workforce;
- hiring new AI and data talent;
- acquihiring;
- partnering with external providers and accessing AI-as-a-service solutions.

It's likely you'll need a combination of these strategies, rather than relying on one single approach. But let's explore each option briefly.

### UPSKILLING YOUR EXISTING WORKFORCE

Given the explosion in AI and big data, there's a severe shortage in data analysts and AI talent. And what talent there is tends to be hoovered up by giants like Google, Apple, Microsoft, IBM, and so on. For everyone else, attracting the right talent is a real challenge.

That's why upskilling existing employees is a good idea for many employers. For example, there is a wealth of massive open online courses

(MOOCs) designed to help develop skills related to AI and data science. However, it's also important to build hands-on experience, which can be done by pairing learners with more experienced colleagues or mentors.

### HIRING NEW AI AND DATA TALENT

Hiring in AI and data skills can be expensive – and difficult, given the scarcity of talent. If you are looking to bridge the skills gap through hiring, it's vital you define a clear USP that makes in-demand talent want to work for your company. Are you, for example, working to solve major problems, make the world a better place, improve people's lives, or achieve other outcomes that candidates find valuable?

### ACQUIHIRING

Very often, hiring talent or upskilling the existing workforce aren't realistic options. In which case, you have to start looking outside the organization for skills and capabilities. Acquihiring (a mashup of 'acqui-sition' and 'hiring') is proving a popular solution for many businesses.

The term refers to the emerging trend where companies who need to boost their AI skills simply acquire small AI or tech startups. By buying up a small startup, the acquirer gets quick access to data engineers and scientists who have experience building and training AI models – thereby accelerating their AI progress.

However, as with any acquisition, there are pitfalls to this approach. An MIT study found that a whopping 33 per cent of acqui-hired talent leave in the first year after purchase,[12] which demonstrates the importance of managing the transition carefully and looking for acquisitions that are a good cultural fit with your own organization.

### PARTNERING WITH EXTERNAL PROVIDERS AND ACCESSING AI-AS-A-SERVICE SOLUTIONS

Another option for tapping into external skills is to partner with companies who have the required skills, or pay for AI-as-a-Service (AIaaS) solutions. I briefly touched on AIaaS in Chapter 5. In a nutshell, the term refers to third parties that offer ready-made AI tools, allowing pretty much any business to take advantage of AI without investing in expensive infrastructure or new hires.

There are lots of AI provider platforms out there, with some of the best-known being:

- IBM Watson
- Amazon Web Services
- Google Cloud platform
- Microsoft Azure

Platforms like these lower the barriers to entry for companies looking to take advantage of AI, without having to hire a team of in-house data scientists or acquire smaller companies for their AI capabilities.

Another way to access external skills is to set up a tech 'incubator' or innovation hub, which can be a good way for companies outside the tech industry to gain access to talent and foster collaborations with AI experts. For example, brewer AB InBev – the world's largest brewer, and makers of Budweiser, Stella Artois and Corona – has created a Silicon Valley innovation hub, called the 'Beer Garage' to explore how cutting-edge technologies like AI can help drive performance. The Beer Garage is designed to help the company research, develop and test technology-driven solutions – but also puts the company in close proximity to the vast network of tech companies and venture capitalists in the Silicon Valley area. This fosters collaboration with local startups and helps to drive innovation. The company says it's learning a lot from working with these inspiring tech experts.[13]

## Building the right soft skills

Technical skills and data literacy are obviously important in the intelligence revolution, but we also need to focus on building skills in areas that robots can't do well – the human side of work. When we talk about AI skills, these softer skills are often overlooked. But in fact they represent a key part of preparing for and succeeding in the intelligence revolution. As robots, computers and machines take on more of the mundane, repetitive and easily automated aspects of work, what's left for humans are those tasks that require a different skillset: things like creativity. Therefore, if the work of humans is going to become altogether more human, it makes sense that we should be developing those skills that make us uniquely human. But what skills are we talking about exactly?

## Nine soft skills every organization and employee must focus on

Don't let the name fool you. In the intelligence revolution, the following 'soft' skills are going to be hard currency indeed.

### CREATIVITY

Robots currently can't compete with humans when it comes to our ability to invent, create, imagine and dream. In the future, human workers will need to harness creative thinking if they're to fully realize the benefits of all the new things coming our way (new products, new technology, new ways of working, etc). In other words, the workplaces of the future will require new ways of thinking, and I believe human creativity is the key to it.

### EMOTIONAL INTELLIGENCE

Also known as EQ (like an emotional IQ), emotional intelligence describes a person's ability to be aware of, control and express their own emotions as well as being aware of the emotions of others. Having empathy, demonstrating integrity and working well with others are all signs of a high EQ. And because machines can't easily replace our ability to really connect with other human beings, those with high EQs will be in even greater demand in the future.

### ANALYTICAL (CRITICAL) THINKING

Those with critical thinking skills can come up with innovative solutions and ideas, solve complex problems using reasoning and logic (rather than relying on emotion or gut feeling) and evaluate arguments. They can weigh up the pros and cons of a situation and remain open-minded as to the best possible solutions. As we navigate the changing division of labour between humans and machines, this ability to think analytically will be all the more precious.

### ACTIVE LEARNING WITH A GROWTH MINDSET

AI will accelerate the learning need for workers, as skills will become outdated much faster than they do today. A person with a growth mindset understands that their abilities and intelligence can be developed and they know that their effort to build skills will result in higher achievement. These people take on new challenges, learn from mistakes and actively seek to expand their knowledge – vital for the future of work.

And at an organizational level, companies must create an active learning environment that embraces continual learning.

## JUDGEMENT AND DECISION MAKING

I believe human decision making will become more complex in the future workplace. This might surprise you because machines and data can already process information and provide insights that would be impossible for humans to gather. But ultimately it's humans who are responsible for making the critical decisions in an organization, taking into account the implications of those decisions in terms of other areas of the business, personnel and the effect on other human factors, such as morale. As technology takes away more menial and mundane tasks, it will leave humans to focus on more higher-level decision making. A degree of data literacy will no doubt help humans make these complex decisions and recognize the broader implications.

## INTERPERSONAL COMMUNICATION SKILLS

The ability to exchange information and meaning between people will be a vital skill going forward. Humans must hone their ability to communicate effectively with other human beings so that they are able to say the right things, using the right tone of voice and body language, in order to bring their message across clearly.

## LEADERSHIP SKILLS

Traits we'd commonly associate with leadership – like being inspiring and helping others become the best versions of themselves – will be vital for the future workplace. While it's true that today's typical hierarchical organizational chart might not be as prevalent, and project-based teams and fluid organizational structures may be more commonplace, this doesn't lower the importance of leadership skills. Individuals will still need to take on leadership roles in project teams or work with other employees to tackle issues and develop solutions.

## DIVERSITY AND CULTURAL INTELLIGENCE

The world and workplaces are becoming more diverse and open, which means it's vital individuals have the skills to understand, respect and work with others despite differences in race, culture, language, age, gender, sexual orientation, political or religious beliefs, etc. The ability to understand and adapt to others who might have different ways of perceiving the world will not only improve how people interact within the company, it's likely to make a company's products and services more inclusive and successful, too.

EMBRACING CHANGE

Due to the incredible pace of change, people will have to be agile and able to embrace and celebrate change. Not only will our brains need to be flexible, we'll also need to be adaptable to shifting workplaces, expectations and skillsets. In the intelligence revolution, an essential skill will be the ability to see change not as a burden, but as an opportunity to grow and innovate.

If there's one message you take away from this section, it should be this: the human brain is incredible. It's more powerful and more complex than any AI we can imagine. We needn't be intimidated by AI; instead we should harness our unique human capabilities. Organizations and individuals who can develop in these areas stand themselves in good stead for the future of work.

But success in the age of AI isn't just about soft skills and technical skills. Company culture plays a vital role. It's really important that leaders take everyone with them on this AI journey – addressing people's fears around job augmentation and automation, managing change successfully, and building a workplace that's full of AI advocates.

## Building an AI culture in your organization

For me, creating an AI culture means creating an environment in which all the factors from this chapter come together: preparing people for the changing nature of work; building or accessing the right technical skills and capabilities for success; and building the right soft skills.

### Four steps to prepare for the intelligence revolution

To recap what we've covered so far, if you were to create a simple checklist or roadmap of how to build an AI culture and prepare for the intelligence revolution, it might look something like this:

STEP 1: REDEFINE WORK AND THE ROLE OF PEOPLE IN THE ORGANIZATION

What does work look like in your organization in future? Much of today's work is geared around performing a particular function. But this is likely to change as organizational structures become more fluid. The focus will shift to projects and outcomes rather than particular tasks that need to be repeated over and over again. People in the organization will need to develop the skills and mindset to cope with this, but they can't do it alone – training and support is vital to making sure this transition occurs as smoothly as possible.

STEP 2: IMPROVE TECHNICAL SKILLS

As already discussed, we won't all need to be data scientists or AI experts in the future, but we will *all* need some degree of data literacy. Organizations will need to develop data literacy programmes so that employees are equipped to take advantage of AI and data, and learn to ask questions such as 'How can we use this new technology to drive success and improve performance?', 'How can we ensure we're using it correctly and ethically?' and 'How accurate is the data we're working with?' Organizations will also need to beef up their more advanced technical capabilities, whether that means accessing commercial AI tools that help them make sense of data, or boosting their in-house talent.

STEP 3: DEVELOP HUMAN POTENTIAL

As machines begin to master more tasks typically performed by humans, humans must begin to focus on the areas in which they outperform machines – creative endeavours, imagination, critical thinking, social interaction and so on. Organizational training and education can't afford to overlook these inherent human abilities if the company is to get the very best out of both humans and machines.

STEP 4: REDEFINE LEARNING TO FOCUS ON CONTINUAL LEARNING CYCLES

One report by Dell Technologies and the Institute for the Future predicts that 85 per cent of jobs in 2030 don't exist yet.[14] People will no longer start a career path and only grow with one role, and many of us may be doing very different jobs in a decade's time. Which makes learning all the more important. But not just learning; continual learning. As the world of work continues to evolve, education, learning and training must become a continual endeavour.

## Making the shift to an AI-driven organization

Culture is a key enabler of the AI-driven organization – an organization that is able to successfully harness AI to guide decisions, improve performance, and drive success. With the right culture in place, you enable widespread adoption of AI, right across the business, as opposed to in odd pockets, projects and processes.

It's not a small thing, though, to rewire the entire organizational culture. And it's certainly not an overnight process. Successfully adopting AI requires some serious, long-term shifts. So what sort of longer-term shifts are we talking about? Based on how we believe the world of work will change, companies should look to:

- embrace cross-functional collaboration;
- enable front-line data-driven decision making and action;
- encourage the experimental.

### EMBRACING CROSS-FUNCTIONAL COLLABORATION

The most successful organizations of the future will incorporate AI into their everyday processes and activities, right across the business, which requires a widespread collaborative mindset. To help foster this, you may want to create cross-functional teams that combine IT and data experts with operational workers to solve the company's biggest problems or address strategic priorities using AI.

### ENABLING FRONT-LINE DATA-DRIVEN DECISION MAKING AND ACTION

The goal is to have decision makers at every level of the business using data and AI to augment their decision making, and take positive action based on insights from data. But to do this, you'll need to boost data literacy in the organization (see earlier in the chapter), and ensure teams feel empowered to actually act on those decisions. For example, if everything has to be approved by managers before employees can act on insights, it'll kill off that entrepreneurial spirit pretty quickly.

### ENCOURAGING THE EXPERIMENTAL

In this fast-changing world, I believe the most successful organizations of the future are those in which people are happy to experiment and use data and AI to try new things – even if that means some initiatives fail. Forget the traditionally rigid, risk-averse models of the past; in the future the ability to take risks, fail fast, learn from the experience and move onto new endeavours will become crucial.

## Successfully managing the change

We know that change can be painful, and badly managed change can sap morale, reduce performance, and ultimately hinder adoption of new practices or technologies. Transitioning to an AI-driven organization will require companies to carefully manage change. For me, this means every company must:

- communicate its vision for the AI-powered organization;
- provide reassurance;
- budget carefully for integration;
- deliver quick wins.

### COMMUNICATING YOUR VISION FOR THE AI-POWERED ORGANIZATION

When people don't understand why change is happening, they're much more likely to resist it. It's therefore vital leaders communicate why AI is so important to the organization's success, and how the implementation of AI will benefit people in the organization (for example, automating certain processes frees up individuals to work on more challenging, interesting tasks). Demonstrating the clear link between AI initiatives and the organization's key strategic priorities (see Chapter 7) helps with this, as does showcasing success stories. If you're at the very beginning of your AI journey, you could showcase examples from other companies that have successfully implemented AI.

### PROVIDING REASSURANCE

Many people assume automation will lead to job losses, but as we saw earlier in the chapter, that's not necessarily the case. AI will create more jobs than it displaces. And even for those jobs that are impacted by automation, the likelihood is those jobs will change rather than be lost altogether. Part of 'selling' people on AI is providing reassurance that AI will enhance what they do. Engaging and involving everyone in these discussions will be a key enabler.

### BUDGETING CAREFULLY FOR INTEGRATION

When companies think about the spending associated with adopting AI, they tend to focus on the technology itself or new hires. But you also need to budget for integration and adoption, including training, communication and potentially redesigning practices. In my experience, these adoption-driving activities can take up as much as half of the overall AI budget.

DELIVER QUICK WINS

Shifting towards an AI-driven culture takes time, which can mean enthusiasm drains away and old practices gradually seep back in. That's why, when I work with a company to define their AI strategy, I always recommend they identify one or two AI 'quick wins' (see Chapter 7) – these are smaller projects that aim to demonstrate the value of AI relatively quickly, thereby helping to maintain momentum and enthusiasm for the longer-term shifts.

---

### KEY TAKEAWAYS

In this chapter we've learned:

- AI – particularly automation – is going to transform the way we work. But rather than fear this development or be intimidated by AI, we should embrace this new way of working, where machines take on the boring, mundane tasks that (if we're honest with ourselves) humans aren't best suited to. Therefore, AI gives us an opportunity to make work better.

- It's vital organizations and individuals prepare for the changes that are coming our way. This means building technical skills and capabilities, developing our uniquely human soft skills, and building a company culture that embraces AI.

- When it comes to building technical skills and capabilities, many companies will struggle to bridge the skills gaps. Partnering with external providers and accessing AI-as-a-Service solutions can offer an achievable route to AI.

- While we don't all need to become data scientists in the intelligence revolution, everyone in the organization should look to become more data literate. The objective of data literacy is to give everyone access to the data they need to make better decisions and deliver success. Part of any good data literacy programme should be teaching people to think critically about data and AI, in order to avoid automation bias.

- Our unique human capabilities – things like emotional intelligence, creativity, and the ability to connect and communicate with others – will become more valuable in the intelligence revolution. In the intelligence revolution, these precious soft skills become hard currency.

> • Culture is key to building an AI-powered organization. Those companies that can build a positive AI culture, successfully manage change, and bring everyone along on the AI journey are the ones that will succeed.

Getting the most out of AI isn't just about building the right skills and culture, though. It's vital companies use data and AI ethically, build trust with their customers and employees, and operate in a transparent way. In the next chapter, I explore the ethical implications of the intelligence revolution – and the pitfalls for companies who don't take AI ethics seriously.

## Endnotes

1 PricewaterhouseCoopers (nd) How will automation impact jobs? https://www.pwc.co.uk/services/economics-policy/insights/the-impact-of-automation-on-jobs.html (archived at https://perma.cc/QUK6-5UQR)

2 Reese, B (2019) AI will create millions more jobs than it will destroy. Here's how, *SingularityHub*, https://singularityhub.com/2019/01/01/ai-will-create-millions-more-jobs-than-it-will-destroy-heres-how/amp/ (archived at https://perma.cc/43GS-V6E3)

3 Fingas, J (2019) A digital 'dress' sold for $9,500, *Engadget*, https://www.engadget.com/2019/05/27/fabricant-blockchain-digital-dress/ (archived at https://perma.cc/NH27-C5BU)

4 Capgemini (nd) Artificial intelligence – where and how to invest, https://www.capgemini.com/service/digital-services/insights-data/data-science-analytics/artificial-intelligence-where-and-how-to-invest/ (archived at https://perma.cc/6VYC-GUVV)

5 Marr, B (nd) Instead of destroying jobs artificial intelligence (AI) is creating new jobs in 4 out of 5 companies, https://bernardmarr.com/default.asp?contentID=1194 (archived at https://perma.cc/Y3EY-WJD3)

6 Belton, P (2019) How does it feel to be watched at work all the time? *BBC News*, https://www.bbc.com/news/business-47879798 (archived at https://perma.cc/BYT7-EAJV)

7 Humanyze, https://www.humanyze.com/ (archived at https://perma.cc/52HK-AFHB)

8 Volini, E *et al* (2019) From jobs to superjobs: 2019 Global Human Capital Trends, *Deloitte*, https://www2.deloitte.com/us/en/insights/focus/human-capital-trends/2019/impact-of-ai-turning-jobs-into-superjobs.html (archived at https://perma.cc/2BP3-PVJL)

9 Gaskell, A (2019) The ghost workers powering the AI economy, *Forbes*, https://www.forbes.com/sites/adigaskell/2019/09/02/the-ghost-workers-powering-the-ai-economy/#2ac089bb43eb (archived at https://perma.cc/PX7B-YS5D)

10 PricewaterhouseCoopers (2017) A decade of digital: keeping pace with technology, https://www.pwc.co.uk/consulting/assets/documents/global-2017-digital-iq-report.pdf (archived at https://perma.cc/428Q-PB8B)

11 Whittle, S (2001) The top five internal security threats, *Zdnet*, https://www.zdnet.com/article/the-top-five-internal-security-threats/ (archived at https://perma.cc/N6C2-3Y3B)

12   Somers, M (2019) Your acquired hires are leaving. Here's why, *MIT Sloan School*, https://mitsloan.mit.edu/ideas-made-to-matter/your-acquired-hires-are-leaving-heres-why (archived at https://perma.cc/67QB-SANQ)

13   Marr, B (2019) The amazing ways the brewers of Budweiser are using artificial intelligence to transform the beer industry, *Forbes*, https://www.forbes.com/sites/bernardmarr/2019/09/09/the-amazing-ways-the-brewers-of-budweiser-are-using-artificial-intelligence-to-transform-the-beer-industry/#1e349beb422c (archived at https://perma.cc/55MG-3A5A)

14   Dell Technologies and Institute for the Future (2017) The next era of human-machine partnerships, https://www.delltechnologies.com/content/dam/delltechnologies/assets/perspectives/2030/pdf/SR1940_IFTFforDellTechnologies_Human-Machine_070517_readerhigh-res.pdf (archived at https://perma.cc/9BSF-JY36)

# CHAPTER NINE

# The need for ethics, trust and transparency

How do you feel about companies being able to predict your personality based on who you listen to on Spotify or which bands and artists you like on Facebook? (Already possible, according to psychology researchers.[1]) Sounds harmless enough perhaps. But what about companies accurately predicting your sexual orientation, religious views, intelligence or use of addictive substances based on your Facebook Likes? That's possible, too.[2] Because we now have access to unprecedented amounts of data, suddenly it's possible to easily gain lots of interesting (and sensitive) insights. But just because something is possible, doesn't mean it's right.

Most people are unaware of the amount of highly personal information that can be gleaned about them thanks to data and AI, and the extent to which this technology is already being applied. But that will change. Indeed, as we'll see in this chapter, the 'Wild West' era, where anything goes and the use of AI is barely touched by regulation, is coming to an end. Therefore, for businesses to thrive during the intelligence revolution, I believe they'll have to use AI in an ethical way. They'll have to be transparent about their use of AI and data. And they'll have to develop trusting relationships with their customers and employees.

In this chapter, I explore the ethical pitfalls of AI and make the case for the ethical, AI-driven organizations of the future.

## The dangerous side of AI: how AI can be misused

Like any technology, AI is neutral. It can be used for good, and it can be used for bad. Business leaders looking to use AI ethically need to be aware of the potential ways in which AI is open to misuse. At one end of the scale, we have dodgy practices like not telling people how you intend to use their data, and at the other end, we have technology being used to the detriment of individuals, society and even human life as we know it.

### The AI arms race

Let's start with the scarier end of the scale, and the development of autonomous weapons (as briefly mentioned in Chapter 4). According to a report by peace organization Pax, countries such as the United States, China, the United Kingdom and Russia are accelerating their development of military AI – an AI arms race, if you will.[3] As an example, the report cites the Pentagon's commitment to spending $2 billion across five years to develop 'the next wave of AI technologies'.

Drone swarms – a mass of self-organizing drones that are capable of making decisions among themselves – is one area that governments are particularly keen to develop. DARPA, the US Defense Advanced Research Projects Agency, confirmed in 2018 that it had equipped a squad of drones with the ability to 'adapt and respond to unexpected threats… with minimal communication'.[4] That means, when communications with the human controller were knocked out, the drones were still able to work with each other towards the mission's objective without live human intervention. (It's not just the US that wants to deploy these swarms of drones; the UK government has said British forces will use such 'swarm squadrons' in the future.[5])

But do we really want to develop drone swarms that can make their own tactical decisions, meaning they could, in theory, identify targets and deploy weapons without human intervention? I'm not the only one who thinks the race to develop technology like this – where being the 'first' is perhaps more important than being ethical – is a serious threat to humanity as a whole; influential AI and robotics researchers have signed an open letter calling for a ban on autonomous weapons.[6] In response to such anti-autonomous weapon sentiment – or at least, in acknowledgement of that fact that most people might find the idea of self-organizing weapons vaguely creepy – the Pentagon was, in 2019, looking to recruit an ethicist to oversee military AI.[7]

### Worryingly convincing fakes

We hear a lot about fake news and deepfakes these days. But, in my experience, few people understand just how clever the technology is, and how serious a threat this poses to us all.

In Chapter 2, I referred to Baidu's technology, which can clone someone's voice from three seconds of audio. We've also had deepfake porn videos circulating online featuring celebrities such as Scarlett Johansson, with the actor's face convincingly fused with the body of a porn actor. The now defunct DeepNude app allowed users to take an image of a fully clothed woman and remove her clothes – creating non-consensual porn. Deepfake videos of President Barack Obama and Mark Zuckerberg show how it's possible to create a video of someone saying whatever you want. And a doctored video of US House Speaker Nancy Pelosi drunkenly stumbling over her words was retweeted as real by President Donald Trump in 2019.[8] Software exists that allows users to edit the transcript of a video to alter the words coming out of the speaker's mouth, simply by typing what you want them to say.[9] With Stanford University's Deep Video Portraits system, it's possible to animate a picture of someone, manipulating the subject's facial expressions and making their head move.[10] And an AI system built by OpenAI is now able to generate fake news that is apparently so good its creators refuse to release the full model for wider experimentation, considering it too dangerous and open to 'malicious applications'.[11]

Worryingly, Gartner predicts that, by 2022, we'll consume more lies than truth.[12] It's already getting harder and harder to discern what's real and what's artificial, and the fact that your voice can be cloned with just a few seconds of audio should give us all pause for thought. In other words, the same sort of technology that allows you to harmlessly programme your Google Assistant to speak with a celebrity's voice, could be used against you.

We all need to raise our awareness of what technology is capable of, and how sophisticated it is. And we all need to be a little more critical when it comes to assessing information and verifying its validity before we act on it. (Circle back to Chapter 8 for more on critical thinking.)

There is hope that, as well as enabling this fake content, AI may also help humans detect deepfakes in the future. Scientists at the University of Washington have created an AI system called GROVER that's capable of creating very believable fake news articles based only on a headline – but it's not designed to fill the internet with propaganda; according to the team who built it, it's the most effective defence against fake news and can detect fake articles better than any other existing tool.[13] That's certainly encouraging, but only if the technology never falls into the wrong hands.

### Using AI to exploit people

Finally, it's not just governments and bored ne'er-do-wells we should be concerned about. There are plenty of corporations out there who have used AI to exploit their customers and users to the max, rather than thinking about how AI could benefit the customer. One example is the use of AI in gambling websites, where the AI can be used to predict users' behaviour and encourage them to spend more and more money – money they may not have. Essentially, the AI is about getting and keeping people hooked, rather than providing a better, more valuable service to users.[14]

For me, a big part of the ethical use of AI means using AI and data to provide real value for customers, users and employees. If you can do that, you'll be encouraging greater loyalty anyway, without needing to 'trick' or 'trap' people. But being an ethical AI company also means being transparent with people about how you're using AI and data – an area in which many a high-profile company has failed in the past. Which brings me to…

## The days of trampling over individual privacy and being less than transparent are over

Any company that I work with, I always advise them to be transparent about how they're using AI and data. In the long run, an ethical, transparent approach will add genuine value to the business and help to build trust with customers and other stakeholders – particularly as people gradually become more aware of unethical uses of AI.

## Facebook provides a lesson to us all

One useful warning tale comes from Facebook's Beacon programme, which hoovered up data from various external sites and posted users' online purchases from those sites to their Facebook wall. The general idea was to help promote retailers. The trouble was, by and large, users had no idea that Facebook was gathering that data and would be posting it on their wall. Most examples were relatively harmless, if invasive – like the woman who bought a coffee table from Overstock, and then saw the purchase was added to her Facebook wall – but in one example a guy ordered a diamond ring online, only for Facebook to broadcast his impending proposal to all his friends and family... and girlfriend.[15] Facebook has since stopped the programme, and been ordered to pay a $9.5 million settlement for breaching privacy laws.[16]

Facebook has come under increasing pressure to be more privacy-conscious in the wake of the Cambridge Analytica scandal. So it's perhaps no surprise that, in 2019, Facebook announced it was changing its use of facial recognition technology. The technology, which was used to autotag people in photos, is now finally an opt-in setting that users have to turn on.[17] Facebook's decision comes after it lost an appeal case concerning the company's use of facial recognition data. The appeal court's ruling, that 'the development of a face template using facial recognition technology without consent invades an individual's private affairs,'[18] potentially opens the company up to hefty damages payments for not gaining users' consent to gather their facial data.

As an aside, the wider use of facial recognition technology, which is underpinned by AI, is an area that makes many people wary, prompting some cities to ban it.[19] Despite the advantages facial recognition brings to policing and security, many feel the technology is a threat to individual privacy. The potential disadvantages of facial recognition shouldn't be underestimated. For one thing, the technology has in some cases been better at identifying white males than people of colour and women, leading to concerns that it could misidentify people.[20] With concerns over accuracy as well as privacy, lawmakers are now calling for regulation of facial recognition technology.[21]

## Even our homes are no longer as private as we thought

Customers with certain smart home gadgets were outraged in 2019 when it emerged real-life people were listening to their Alexa and Google

Assistant requests. Both Amazon and Google admitted that contractors are hired to listen to anonymized audio clips from Alexa and Google Assistant devices – which, to many customers, sounded like 'spying'. Both companies stressed contractors were only listening in order to improve the smart assistants' capabilities, for example, by training speech recognition systems. Yet the fact remains customers generally had no clue that humans might listen in to their audio data.

Amazon has also raised more than a few eyebrows among privacy advocates with its recent patent application. The company's design for a smart doorbell that uses a camera to monitor the neighbourhood and report suspicious activity to the police sounds pretty disturbing to me.[22] Does anyone like the idea of their neighbour's doorbell spying on them? Particularly for those who choose not to use Amazon or have smart products in the home, the fact that an Amazon device *next door* could be gathering information on their activities is unpalatable to say the least.

Of course, the truth is our smart home devices are gathering so much data on us all the time. So is Google. So are the websites we visit. So are our phones. Generally speaking, it's not necessarily the gathering or use of that data that's the problem; consumer backlash tends to occur when people were previously unaware their data was being used that way, and were given no choice to opt in or out. (Like people who just happen to live next door to someone with a smart doorbell!)

The privacy tides are turning, though. At the time of writing, Amazon had just introduced a 'no human review' option to its Alexa settings, which allows users to opt out of their audio being manually reviewed by human workers.[23] Settings like this will become more commonplace as consumers become ever-more conscious of privacy issues. To put it another way, companies can no longer assume they have free rein to hoover up people's data (be it audio data, face data, online activity data or whatever) and apply AI to that data. Going forward, companies will have to be 100 per cent transparent on how they're using data and AI, and ensure they get customer consent for that use.

## The 'black box' problem: or, how we don't really understand how AI works

More and more everyday decisions are being supported by AI – from the spellchecker that's correcting my typos as I write this chapter, to the satnav I follow in my car. We place a lot of trust in these systems, allowing them to direct our decision making and activities without really thinking about *how* the system is doing what it's doing. AI is like sausages in that way – most of us would rather not know how the sausage gets made, we just want to eat it!

## What goes on inside the box?

The trouble is, even when we do want to understand how an AI decision was made, we might not be able to get an explanation. That's because we can't always understand how AIs make the decisions they do, especially very advanced deep learning AIs. We feed data into the system, a decision pops out the other end (again, I can't help picturing sausages here), and it's hard to unpack exactly what happens in between. You can't just look under the bonnet of an AI system, in other words. Even AI engineers can't always understand how their own systems work.

If we can't understand how advanced AI algorithms are making decisions, that has serious implications for how we use AI. As an example, European data protection law (GDPR) says that individuals have the right to obtain an explanation of how automated processing systems make decisions that affect them.[24] Say, for example, you've been turned down for a mortgage application on the basis of a decision made by an automated system, GDPR says you have the right to an explanation on *why* you were turned down. If companies can't explain how their systems reach decisions, they're essentially acting unlawfully.

In another example, researchers at New York's Mount Sinai Hospital created a deep learning program that could predict diseases, after learning from the medical records of 700,000 people. The program, called Deep Patient, proved remarkably good at predicting conditions, even successfully predicting the onset of complex psychiatric disorders like schizophrenia – which, considering schizophrenia is notoriously difficult for doctors to predict, had clinicians puzzled.[25] The system offered no rationale at all for its predictions. So, let's say you're a doctor whose patient is predicted to develop schizophrenia. You're faced with a tricky dilemma – do you trust what the system says? Yes, it seems to be very accurate, but you have no way of verifying its prediction in the case of your patient. Do you potentially change a patient's meds on the basis of an unexplainable AI decision? Who will be deemed responsible if the decision is wrong?

## It's a question of trust

This lack of understanding poses huge questions for accountability and trust – as well as accuracy. If we don't understand how something works, how can we identify or predict where it's likely to fail? Should we trust AIs at all if we can't explain their decision-making processes? Or will we find intuitive ways to discern when to trust AIs and when not to (just as we do with humans)? For now, those questions remain unanswered.

The good news is, AI companies appear to be grasping the gravity of the situation. For example, in 2019 IBM announced a new toolkit of algorithms designed to help explain the decisions of deep learning AIs.[26] Called AI 360 Explainability, the toolkit goes some way to interpreting AI decisions, but it's not a magic bullet.

All this is doubly concerning when you consider our human tendency to blindly follow automated systems. This is the 'automation bias' problem I referred to in Chapter 8. For companies to successfully deploy AI, not only will they need to think about the explainability of their automated decisions, they'll need to attune their people to the dangers of automation bias. People need to be trained to not blindly follow automated systems; they must learn to think critically and ask questions about how systems make decisions and what data is used to make those decisions. Increasing general data literacy is therefore an important part of overcoming automation bias – circle back to Chapter 8 for more on automation bias, critical thinking and data literacy.

## Avoiding biased AI

One of the many advantages of AI is that it has the potential to reduce bias. When decisions are augmented or even automated by AI systems, we can remove some of the baggage that humans bring to the decision-making process. One good example is the hiring process. If AI can be used to assess initial applications, then it may serve to eliminate discrimination and improve workplace diversity.

That's the idea, anyway. The reality is that an AI algorithm is only as good as the data it's trained on. If it's trained on biased data, then the AI system will be biased. Let's say I train a basic AI to predict the next president of the United States based only on historical data of past presidents. It's highly likely to predict the next president will be a white man of advancing years! That's because there's a hefty race and gender bias built into the training data.

### Why might data be biased?

Biased data doesn't mean biased data scientists or developers. It's more likely to be an unintentional bias based on a lack of representation – meaning it's probably an inherent systemic bias rather than any one individual's prejudices rearing their head. My fictional database on historic presidents would be one example of systemic bias. Another – real-life – example is the use of flawed systems to assess the risk of defendants reoffending; when one recidivism analytics tool was examined more closely, researchers found that black defendants were much more likely than white defendants to be *incorrectly* judged as having a high risk of reoffending. Meanwhile, white defendants were more likely to be incorrectly judged as low risk.[27]

### Reducing the risk of bias in your organization's data

So what can we do to avoid inherent biases in data? The most obvious way is to check for under- or over-representation in the data being used. You may find you need additional data to correct this. For example, I mentioned earlier in the chapter that facial recognition systems have been found to be better at identifying white men, and not so accurate when it comes to identifying women or people of colour. That's because a widely used data training set for facial recognition systems was estimated to be more than 75 per cent male and 80 per cent white – something that programmers were easily able to correct by adding a more diverse range of faces to the training dataset.[28]

It's also vital people learn to think critically about the decisions being enhanced or automated through AI, and not blindly follow them. This further emphasizes the need to improve data literacy and critical thinking skills in every organization (Chapter 8).

The consequences of not addressing biases in data can be serious. You could be looking at inaccurate decisions, or loss of reputation and trust – outcomes that are bad enough for any organization. But, depending on your industry, the consequences can be far graver. Just imagine what happens if patient treatment decisions are based on biased or incomplete datasets. It's not hard to imagine there could be serious legal ramifications, too.

## Problems around AI security and hacking

In Chapter 6, I highlighted how AI can be used to improve IT security and detect phishing scams. Unfortunately, AI and automation can also be used to the hackers' advantage. For example, AI bots can be used to automatically trawl the internet to find sites that have security issues, and AI-driven tools can be used to automatically perform multiple ransomware attacks at a time. In other words, thanks to AI, attacks will become cheaper and easier to deploy than ever before.

Technology has always been open to malicious use, that's nothing new. But the rapid advancement of AI technologies means we may be facing dramatically more sophisticated threats, and sooner than we think. Phishing, for example, is likely to become much harder to detect. Phishing relies on realistic-seeming messages designed to trick people into visiting a fake website and giving up their security details. In theory, AI could be used to make these messages all the more realistic. Imagine a fake message from your partner asking you to remind them of the login details for your joint bank account – AI could make that message read just like something your partner would write. Sound far-fetched? Just think how realistic chatbot technology is already, and how hard it is to tell a bot from a human. We also know that it's increasingly easy to generate fake content, including fake audio and video. It's not unthinkable to imagine that hackers could fake, say, an IT colleague's voice and use that to trick employees into giving up system passwords.

The very technology that's helping to improve IT security could be co-opted by the very people organizations are trying to defend against. So what should organizations do to help protect themselves? I hope it goes without saying that all organizations need a robust, regularly updated IT security policy. But, for me, awareness is always the first line of defence. Organizations must be aware of the ever-changing threat landscape, and they must work hard to educate employees on potential threats and ensure everyone is aware of the company's security policies.

## Facing up to the climate impact of AI

AI is a power-hungry beast. Not in a grubby political way, of course. In an energy-usage way.

When it comes to discussing AI and ethics, few people raise the link between AI and energy usage. Yes, AI-driven tools like smart thermostats can help us all be more energy efficient, and that's great. But we also shouldn't forget the fact that AI requires enormous computing power to work, which in turn requires enormous amounts of electricity. And given the fact that much of our energy today is still derived from coal and oil, it means AI has a huge carbon footprint.

Advances like cloud computing and AI-as-a-service make this an easy thing to overlook. When you're outsourcing data storage to the cloud and using cloud-based software, it's all too easy to ignore the energy involved. After all, you don't need a complex data centre to power your analytics – it lives in the cloud. But the cloud isn't an abstract concept. It's real, and it relies on computing power to function. It's just that you're using other people's computing power – Microsoft's, say, or Amazon's – rather than your own.

The irony is that some of the biggest employers in the world, some of the most environmentally conscious companies, with their high-tech, low-impact buildings and campuses are guzzling electricity through their use of AI. What sort of impact are we talking about? Training an AI system can create 17 times more carbon emissions than the average American does in a year.[29] And since 2012, the amount of computational power needed to train AI systems has been doubling every 3.5 months.[30] As a result of this startling growth, it's predicted that AI could account for one-tenth of the world's electricity usage by 2025.[31]

(Just think what we could achieve if we applied this energy to solving some of the world's biggest problems, like cancer, or poverty, or the spread of malaria, or the lack of affordable healthcare for all, or the impact of climate change…)

The truth is, now that AI is an increasingly realistic option for most businesses – big or small – there's no going back. Technological advancement only goes one way, and there's no doubt in my mind that the most successful businesses of the future will be AI-driven organizations. So my message here isn't to avoid AI because of the amount of energy it uses; rather, I think we should all be a little more aware of the energy AI uses. Businesses should also hold their cloud providers to account for their energy usage. As part of this, the big tech giants need to be much more upfront about the toll AI takes on the planet.

I also believe all organizations must learn to prioritize the use of AI. In other words, just because something can be analysed or automated through AI, doesn't mean it *should* be. Part of using AI ethically is using it where it counts most – where it delivers most benefit for your business and your stakeholders.

## The ethical human–robot relationship

Allow me to get slightly more futuristic for a moment. As AI robots become a more common part of everyday life and work, it's worth considering our relationship with the robots of the future – and how our interactions with robots may, in fact, change the way humans interact with each other.

Writing in the *Atlantic*, sociology professor Nicholas Christakis described his experiments at Yale, in which the presence of a robotic co-worker helped humans be more relaxed and collaborative with each other. Groups paired with a perky robot that freely acknowledged and apologized for (deliberately programmed) mistakes during tasks were found to communicate and collaborate better with each other.[32] Conversely, another of Christakis's experiments demonstrated that robots playing an online game in a selfish way made otherwise generous human players behave in a similarly selfish way. The presence of robots can, therefore, impact the way humans behave – which is an interesting point for employers to consider.

Looking even further ahead, as robots potentially become more life-like, and more capable of carrying out human-like thought processes, will there come a point when robots cease being machines and become a new lifeform? And if that happens, how will humans and robots interact then? What rights will robots be entitled to? How can we ensure robotic colleagues are treated in an ethical, fair way? It's certainly interesting food for thought. But, for now, let's set aside my Blade Runner-esque imaginings and focus on the here and now. What should your organization be doing to ensure AI is used ethically? Let's find out.

## Putting it all into practice: using AI ethically in your business

The lawsuits against Facebook mentioned earlier in the chapter show how the public is beginning to wake up to the ethical issues surrounding AI. This public awareness and potential for backlash is only going to increase – and policy makers and regulators will no doubt take an increasing interest in AI – making it vital you pursue an ethical use of AI.

For me, this means organizations must:

- build a relationship of trust with customers and employees;
- avoid the black box problem;
- think critically;
- check for data bias.

Let's briefly recap each area in turn.

### Building trust

Organizations must be transparent with customers, employees and other stakeholders about how they're using AI and data. You could argue that companies like Facebook haven't been very good at this so far and have perhaps tried to get away with things without telling users what they're doing. As regulators begin to scrutinize the big tech giants more and more, emulating this less-than-transparent approach is a dangerous path to go down. Far better to be up front about what data you gather, how that data is analysed, and why – and all in a straightforward manner, as opposed to burying the details in long, jargon-heavy terms and conditions that nobody reads.

As well as being transparent, ethical AI-driven businesses should also seek informed consent for gathering people's data and, wherever possible, give people the choice to opt out.

Another key part of building trust is value. The AI-driven organization isn't about exploiting people, or wringing every last penny out of consumers. It's about adding real value wherever possible. Therefore, think about how AI can help you create better products, deliver a smarter service, solve your customers' problems, improve the working lives of employees, and so on. People are generally happy for their data to be used when it's clear they're getting something valuable in return.

### Avoiding the black box problem

If you can't explain how an AI system reaches its decisions, think twice. Organizations must think to question AI providers and experts for details of how their AI does what it does. If they can't explain it to you, how would you explain it to your stakeholders? And how would you know to trust those decisions? Wherever possible, look for AI tools that promote explainability, like the IBM toolkit I mentioned earlier in the chapter.

## Thinking critically

Just because AI can enhance or automate decision making, that doesn't mean we should abdicate all decision making to machines. Quite the opposite. As more decisions are being driven by AI, the need for humans to think critically about AI systems is more important than ever. In practice, this means educating people in the organization about AI, and encouraging them to question AI decisions (data involved, how decisions are made, etc). It's really important to give people the tools they need to overcome automation bias (see Chapter 8).

## Checking for biases in data and algorithms

Organizations must consider the data used to train their AI systems – particularly whether that data over- or under-represents certain factors – and the potential for bias in algorithms. Granted, it takes an expert eye to examine data and AI algorithms in any real depth, but that doesn't get non-techies off the hook. Organizations must think to ask these questions of AI providers, rather than blindly trusting that data and AI algorithms are unbiased.

## Making use of available best practice guidelines

In addition to the tips set out above, I'm pleased to say there are some excellent best practice guidelines and organizations out there promoting the responsible use of AI. In particular, I would highly recommend:

- **Partnership on AI.**[33] This partnership is working to shape best practices, research and public dialogue around AI. Members include companies like Amazon and Google, media organizations like the BBC, and non-profit organizations such as Unicef.
- *US Leadership in AI,* published by NIST (National Institute of Standards and Technology).[34] More of a high-level roadmap for developing AI standards than a set of clear-cut rules, but it does set out potential initiatives to promote the responsible use of AI. Useful for a birds-eye view of where AI standards might be going in future.

- *Ethics Guidelines for Trustworthy AI*, published by the European Commission.[35] These guidelines set out key requirements that AI systems must meet in order to be deemed trustworthy.
- *Principles on AI,* published by the OECD (Organization for Economic Co-operation and Development).[36] Personally, this is my favourite set of AI guidelines, and I would strongly advise all companies to follow these best practice international AI standards. OECD's guidance has been officially adopted by 42 countries.

In brief, the OECD's principles for the responsible use of AI state that:

- AI should benefit people and the planet.
- AI should be designed in a way that respects the law, human rights, democratic values and diversity.
- There should be transparency, so that people can understand and challenge AI-based outcomes.
- AI must function in a robust, secure and safe way – with risks being continually assessed and managed.
- Organizations deploying AI should be held accountable for their proper functioning, in line with these principles.

Finally, I must stress that this is just the beginning for AI oversight, and we can expect new standards will emerge in time. It's therefore vital organizations stay up to date on changing best practice and legislation.

---

### KEY TAKEAWAYS

In this chapter we've learned:

- Being an ethical AI company means using AI and data to provide real value for customers, users and employees.
- It's vital your business is 100 per cent transparent with customers, employees and other stakeholders on how you're using data and AI.
- Explainability is a key challenge companies will need to address, as we don't necessarily know exactly how complex AIs work. Your people must therefore learn to think critically about AI systems and question how AIs make decisions.
- AI is only as good as the data it uses, so beware of biases in your data.

- Security is another key challenge, since AI can be used to increase the sophistication, ease and proliferation of attacks. It's vital you create and maintain a robust security strategy and raise awareness of threats.
- Be sure to stay up to date on the latest best practice guidance and emerging legislation.

Ethical issues and potential AI risks aren't the only obstacles companies will need to overcome on their AI journey. Finding the right data for AI can be a challenge for some businesses. In the next chapter I look at the relationship between AI and data – and set out how to gather or access the valuable data you need.

## Endnotes

1  Nave, G *et al* (2018) Musical preferences predict personality: evidence from active listening and Facebook likes, *Psychological Science*, https://journals.sagepub.com/doi/abs/10.1177/0956797618761659 (archived at https://perma.cc/2BUU-XJPF)

2  Kosinski, M, Stillwell, D and Graepel, T (2013) Private traits and attributes are predictable from digital records of human behaviour, *Proceedings of the National Academy of Sciences of the United States of America*, https://www.pnas.org/content/110/15/5802.full (archived at https://perma.cc/R4US-TTJS)

3  Pax (nd) State of AI: Artificial intelligence, the military, and increasingly autonomous weapons, http://www.reprogrammingwar.org/ (archived at https://perma.cc/DX2G-Z2LG)

4  DARPA (2018) CODE Demonstrates Autonomy and Collaboration with Minimal Human Commands, https://www.darpa.mil/news-events/2018-11-19 (archived at https://perma.cc/3R9Q-5E7U)

5  McMullan, T (2019) How swarming drones will change warfare, *BBC News*, https://www.bbc.com/news/technology-47555588 (archived at https://perma.cc/7RBU-UE3H)

6  Future of Life Institute (2015) Autonomous weapons: An open letter from AI & robotics researchers, https://futureoflife.org/open-letter-autonomous-weapons/ (archived at https://perma.cc/UQ7V-M42N)

7  Smith, D (2019) Pentagon seeks 'ethicist' to oversee military AI, *Guardian*, https://www.theguardian.com/us-news/2019/sep/07/pentagon-military-artificial-intelligence-ethicist# (archived at https://perma.cc/589C-KNLU)

8  Reuters (2019) Trump retweets doctored video of Pelosi to portray her as having 'lost it', https://www.reuters.com/article/us-usa-trump-pelosi/trump-retweets-doctored-video-of-pelosi-to-portray-her-as-having-lost-it-idUSKCN1SU2CB (archived at https://perma.cc/LLP3-6B94)

9   Vincent, J (2019) AI deepfakes are now as simple as typing whatever you want your subject to say, *The Verge*, https://www.theverge.com/2019/6/10/18659432/deepfake-ai-fakes-tech-edit-video-by-typing-new-words (archived at https://perma.cc/32HA-2BLM)

10  Stanford University (2018) Deep Video Portraits

11  Wakefield, J (2019) 'Dangerous' AI offers to write fake news, *BBC News*, https://www.bbc.com/news/technology-49446729 (archived at https://perma.cc/JMQ5-WXTY)

12  Panetta, K (2017) Gartner top strategic predictions for 2018 and beyond, *Gartner*, https://www.gartner.com/smarterwithgartner/gartner-top-strategic-predictions-for-2018-and-beyond/ (archived at https://perma.cc/8WY7-5GGQ)

13  Robitzski, D (2019) New AI generates horrifyingly plausible fake news, *Futurism*, https://futurism.com/ai-generates-fake-news (archived at https://perma.cc/A6XR-8L8R)

14  Busby, M (2018) Revealed: how bookies use AI to keep gamblers hooked, *Guardian*, https://www.theguardian.com/technology/2018/apr/30/bookies-using-ai-to-keep-gamblers-hooked-insiders-say (archived at https://perma.cc/9T5A-EK76)

15  CNN Money (2010) 5 data breaches: From embarrassing to deadly, https://money.cnn.com/galleries/2010/technology/1012/gallery.5_data_breaches/3.html (archived at https://perma.cc/7VBT-QJWQ)

16  Kravets, D (2010) Judge approves $9.5 million Facebook 'Beacon' Accord, *Wired*, https://www.wired.com/2010/03/facebook-beacon-2/ (archived at https://perma.cc/6RHN-D7BL)

17  Samuel, S (2019) Facebook will finally ask permission before using facial recognition technology on you, *Vox*, https://www.vox.com/future-perfect/2019/9/4/20849307/facebook-facial-recognition-privacy-zuckerberg (archived at https://perma.cc/PP4D-3EYT)

18  Lecher, C (2019) Facebook could pay billions after losing facial recognition privacy appeal, *The Verge*, https://www.theverge.com/2019/8/8/20792326/facebook-facial-recognition-appeals-decision-damages-payment-court (archived at https://perma.cc/6MRP-6KWJ)

19  Ehrenkranz, M (2019) Another U.S. city moved to ban facial recognition, citing threats to free speech and civil rights, *Gizmodo*, https://gizmodo.com/fourth-u-s-city-bans-facial-recognition-citing-threat-1836858623 (archived at https://perma.cc/R9NV-P485)

20  Marr, B (2019) Facial recognition technology: here are the important pros and cons, *Forbes*, https://www.forbes.com/sites/bernardmarr/2019/08/19/facial-recognition-technology-here-are-the-important-pros-and-cons/#2ea6b09914d1 (archived at https://perma.cc/7VF7-H87H)

21  Dellinger, A (2019) Lawmakers call for regulation of facial recognition tech, *Engadget*, https://www.engadget.com/2019/05/22/congress-committee-facial-recognition-tech-regulation/ (archived at https://perma.cc/8RAN-6VTS)

22  Christian, J (2018) A New Amazon camera patent is straight out of "1984", *Futurism*, https://futurism.com/new-amazon-patent-1984 (archived at https://perma.cc/R4ZF-8RXN)

23  Lomas, N (2019) Amazon quietly adds 'no human review' option to Alexa settings as voice AIs face privacy scrutiny, *TechCrunch*, https://techcrunch.com/2019/08/03/amazon-quietly-adds-no-human-review-option-to-alexa-as-voice-ais-face-privacy-scrutiny/ (archived at https://perma.cc/7APC-RVF6)

24   De la Torre, L (2019) The 'right to an explanation' under EU data protection law, *Medium*, https://medium.com/golden-data/what-rights-related-to-automated-decision-making-do-individuals-have-under-eu-data-protection-law-76f70370fcd0 (archived at https://perma.cc/7P27-BBXR)

25   Knight, W (2017) The dark secret at the heart of AI, *Technology Review*, https://www.technologyreview.com/s/604087/the-dark-secret-at-the-heart-of-ai/ (archived at https://perma.cc/C8WG-G92T)

26   Ray, T (2019) IBM offers explainable AI toolkit, but it's open to interpretation, *ZDNet*, https://www.zdnet.com/article/ibm-offers-explainable-ai-toolkit-but-its-open-to-interpretation/#ftag=CAD-03-10abf5f (archived at https://perma.cc/3VUL-RJVK)

27   Larson, J *et al* (2016) How we analyzed the COMPAS recidivism algorithm, *ProPublica*, https://www.propublica.org/article/how-we-analyzed-the-compas-recidivism-algorithm (archived at https://perma.cc/69VC-JU3G)

28   Taulli, T (2019) How bias distorts AI, *Forbes*, https://www.forbes.com/sites/tomtaulli/2019/08/04/bias-the-silent-killer-of-ai-artificial-intelligence/#260abf2e7d87 (archived at https://perma.cc/V5AU-WEKP)

29   Vanjani, K (2019) The rise of artificial intelligence comes with rising needs for power, *MarketWatch*, https://www.marketwatch.com/story/the-rise-of-artificial-intelligence-comes-with-rising-needs-for-power-2019-08-21 (archived at https://perma.cc/T43X-WA2G)

30   OpenAI (2018) AI and Compute, https://openai.com/blog/ai-and-compute/ (archived at https://perma.cc/5Y7F-C5JQ)

31   Giles, M (2019) Is AI the next big climate-change threat? We haven't a clue, *Technology Review*, https://www.technologyreview.com/s/614005/ai-computing-cloud-computing-microchips/ (archived at https://perma.cc/EM7T-JJZD)

32   Christakis, N (2019) How AI will rewire us, *The Atlantic*, https://www.theatlantic.com/magazine/archive/2019/04/robots-human-relationships/583204/ (archived at https://perma.cc/P47K-JPNR)

33   Partnership on AI, https://www.partnershiponai.org/partners/ (archived at https://perma.cc/7XV8-PA34)

34   NIST (2019) U.S. leadership in AI, https://www.nist.gov/system/files/documents/2019/08/10/ai_standards_fedengagement_plan_9aug2019.pdf (archived at https://perma.cc/85WZ-7VQW)

35   European Commission (2019) Ethics guidelines for trustworthy AI, https://ec.europa.eu/digital-single-market/en/news/ethics-guidelines-trustworthy-ai (archived at https://perma.cc/2VAP-KRVV)

36   OECD (2019) OECD Principles on AI, https://www.oecd.org/going-digital/ai/principles/ (archived at https://perma.cc/JF34-JMHT)

# CHAPTER TEN

# AI needs data (lots of data)

Intelligent machines are very data hungry. Which means, without data, we wouldn't have AI as we know it. Many of the latest breakthroughs in machine learning (see Chapter 2) came from data – or, more specifically, the fact that we have more data than ever before.

Therefore, in the intelligence revolution, data has become a vital business asset. For some businesses, it's the most important asset they have. Yet data presents a challenge for many businesses – what sort of data do you need and how can you access or generate that data? In this chapter, we'll explore AI's need for huge datasets (basically, collections of data) and how to get your hands on the data you need to make your business more intelligent.

Data isn't exactly the liveliest subject. It can often be dry and overly technical, but don't be tempted to skip this chapter. Here, I aim to make the subject as accessible and engaging as possible – ensuring you don't need a background in data science to understand and get the most out of data.

## Revisiting the incredible growth in data

The fact that AI algorithms are so data-hungry can seem daunting, but business leaders can take heart from the fact that they already have so much more data than they've ever had before. What's more, having a limited dataset may be much less of an obstacle than you think…

## The acceleration of data

The vast majority of data we have today was created very recently. In fact, 90 per cent of the data available in the world today was generated in the last two years.[1] We're also doubling the amount of data we have available every two years.[2] Big data is getting bigger, essentially. So much so that market intelligence company IDC estimates that the amount of data in the world could grow from 33 zettabytes in 2018 to 175 zettabytes in 2025.[3] That's a lot of data. Try to store 175 zettabytes on DVDs and you'd have yourself a stack of DVDs so high it could encircle Earth 222 times.

What really excites me is we're currently only analysing a tiny fraction of the data that's available to us. AI makes the process of analysing even complex, unwieldy data (such as video data) much easier and quicker. So as AI gets smarter, we'll be able to capitalize even more on the massive amounts and different types of data being generated.

But where is all this data coming from? In Chapter 2 I outlined how even simple everyday activities are producing data – even something as analogue as going for a walk generates data, if you're carrying your mobile phone, taking pictures on your walk, or wearing a fitness tracker. When you think about the increasing digitization of our lives, it's perhaps not so surprising that the amount of data we're generating is doubling every two years.

In just one minute on the internet in 2019:[4]

- 1 million people logged into Facebook;
- Google received 3.8 million search requests;
- 188 million emails were sent;
- 4.5 million YouTube videos were watched;
- over 40 million messages were sent on WhatsApp and Messenger.

And that's just in one minute.

## Why we might not need so much data in the future

Interestingly, although AI gives us greater opportunities to make sense of data, it may also mean that we need less data in future. Confused? As AI becomes more intelligent, it'll come to rely on fewer data samples.

Currently, AI needs massive datasets to learn from (this is known as training data). But, over time, AIs will get better at learning from more limited training data. AIs will get better at general reasoning and be able to understand concepts based on smaller amounts of data, just as humans do. Here's an example: let's say you show someone a picture of a domesticated cat for the first time, then show them a picture of a lynx. They'll most likely recognize the lynx as a type of cat, without needing to be told all the different types of cats in existence. Humans' innate intelligence and reasoning means we can apply the general concept of a cat to other types of cats (and solve other, more pressing problems, of course).

Compare that to today's AIs, which need to be trained on masses of data to be accurate and can be quite easily thrown by less familiar situations. (One brilliant example being the iPhone X's facial recognition system's inability to recognize 'morning faces' – that puffy, tired look many of us sport when we first get up.[5]) But, over time, AIs will get better at the sort of general reasoning that humans excel at – which, in turn, will reduce the need for massive training datasets.

Two developments will play a major role in the reduced need for data: reinforcement learning and generative adversarial networks (GANs). *Reinforcement learning* essentially means letting AIs learn for themselves through a process of trial and error, rather than being taught by human programmers, which allows AIs to come up with previously unimagined solutions to problems (see also Chapter 2). And *GANs*, in very simple terms, involve pairing up two networks that compete against each other to enhance their understanding. For example, when it comes to recognizing cats in pictures, one network could be working to separate fake cat pictures from real cat pictures, while a 'competing' network could be creating images that look like cats but aren't, in an attempt to fool the first network. Through this process, both networks become better at understanding the general concept of a cat – and because the system is generating its own believable pictures of cats, it doesn't need as much 'real-world' data to learn from.

Therefore, in the future, we're likely to see enhanced reasoning and common sense in machines, allowing them to generalize from fewer examples. In other words, right now AI is nothing without data. But that won't always be the case, as artificial intelligence becomes more like, well, *real* intelligence. And this reduced need for data will hopefully make AI even more accessible for businesses.

## What type and how much data do you need?

There's no rule of thumb that works for all businesses, unfortunately. How much data you need and the type of data you need will depend on what you're trying to achieve. The amount of data required will depend on how complex a problem you're looking to solve, and we also need to remember that different data is required for different analytic methods. (Video data for a computer vision system, for instance, or conversation data for a natural language processing system.)

The following guiding principles will help you assess your data needs:

- your data must be linked to your AI strategy;
- remember to look beyond traditional data types;
- the 'rule of 10' can help determine data quantity.

Let's explore each point in turn.

### Your data needs should be driven by your AI strategy

We know data is an important business asset. But I've noticed a worrying trend towards some IT vendors pushing companies to collect every data point they can, and never waste any data. That's fine if you have the unlimited resources of a company like Google, but the vast majority of companies simply don't need to collect everything they can. Collecting lots of data requires money, skills and infrastructure. Better to focus on the most important data for your business's needs.

This is where your AI strategy comes in (see Chapter 7). Revisit your AI use cases and those priorities will help determine what data you need. If you have the means and opportunity to collect other data beyond those needs – just in case it's useful for the future – then you can consider that. But always start with your strategic needs first.

In other words, you're looking for a balanced approach to data, one that prioritizes data options based on your AI use cases, but that views data as an overall business asset that you want to grow wherever reasonable. This is the approach I take when advising companies on their data needs.

### Looking beyond traditional data

Even today, when we think of data, most of us think of traditional, structured data – like a database. But now there are so many other data options to choose from. We have sound data, image data, text data, activity data, machine-to-machine data, sensor data…

Again, the type of data you need – be it traditional, structured data or complex, unstructured data like video data – depends on the problem you're trying to solve or the decision you're trying to make. When weighing up types of data, it might help to ask yourself:

- **What types of data are relevant to this particular objective?** You can have masses of data at your disposal, but if it doesn't provide meaningful answers in relation to your specific goal or unanswered business questions, it's not very useful.
- **If you could wave a magic wand, what data do you wish you had?** As we'll see later in the chapter, just because you haven't got certain data doesn't mean you can't access it through other means or simulate that data.
- Data diversity is important, so it's likely you'll need to combine data from different sources for the best insights – for example, combining internal data with external data. **So, keeping this in mind, what combination of data sources would best serve your needs?**

### How much data? Introducing the 'rule of 10'

Developing an AI model requires a *training dataset*, which is what's used to train an AI algorithm to perform various tasks or make certain decisions. Currently, training datasets tend to be very large, because it's what the AI learns from.

Estimating the size of a training dataset isn't easy. But, essentially, the more complicated the task, the more data you need – every factor that your AI needs to consider increases the amount of data needed. Many experts use the *rule of 10* as a general rule of thumb. This says you need 10 times as much data as there are degrees of freedom in your model (a degree of freedom might be a parameter that affects the output, or simply a column in a dataset). However, this is only useful as a very quick estimate – simple AI algorithms may require much less data than the rule of 10 implies.

You'll also need a separate *test dataset*, to test how well the AI algorithm does its job, although test datasets tend to be significantly smaller than training datasets.

## How to find the right data

So where does all this data come from? There are many options for sourcing data, with the main ones being:

- collecting new data yourself;
- using publicly available data;
- buying external data;
- crowdsourcing external data;
- augmenting existing data;
- creating synthetic data.

I'll look at each of these options in turn. But before you start to explore options for sourcing new data, the first step is to know what data you already have.

### Auditing your internal data

In my experience, most companies have more data than they realize. It's just that the data may be spread across disparate systems and not really being used to its full advantage. Therefore, understanding what data you already have is a huge step forward.

Your internal data may include:

- transaction histories;
- data on how your customers use your products or services;
- website user activity data;
- finance data;
- HR data;
- data from manufacturing machinery.

Most companies have literally got 1,000s of different data sets.

Your internal data is a particularly rich goldmine because it's so specific to your business. Combined with other data sources (particularly external sources, which I'll come to in a bit), your internal data can provide incredibly detailed and valuable insights.

For example, you can use data on customer purchases and spend to calculate the lifetime value of customers – which gives you the opportunity to focus your marketing spend and activity on those existing customers that bring most value to the business. Combine this knowledge with data from external providers, and you could boost success even further. So, if you know from your internal data that your highest-value customers are over-50s that live within a 10-mile radius of the business (just as an example), you can then use external data, such as social media, to target more customers like that. Or you could use Google Trends data to understand what's trending among your core demographic.

To get the most out of your internal data, you may need to combine your disparate internal sources data into one data location, or create links between the various data silos in your company. This is where it can get technical, so be sure to talk through your options with either an internal data specialist or a data consultant.

Like many companies, you may find your internal data will go some way towards delivering your strategic objectives (see Chapter 7), but it's not quite enough to achieve everything you want. This is when you need to start exploring your options for gathering or accessing new data. Let's look at the key options in turn.

## Collecting data yourself

To supplement your existing internal data, you may want to gather new internal data. This could be as simple as altering the data that feeds into your CRM system, or it could mean, for instance, upgrading your manufacturing machinery to include new sensors.

These days, there are many exciting new methods of collecting data, so whatever data you need, there's a very good chance you'll be able to generate that data. Here are two of my favourite examples of companies thinking outside the box to generate new internal data:

- Cruise operator Royal Caribbean Cruises has invested in some interesting new data collection methods to better understand and improve the customer experience onboard ships. Existing CCTV cameras on ships were retrofitted with smart technology linked to computer vision monitoring systems. Thanks to the data now gathered from CCTV cameras, the company can track footfall as people move around a ship, monitor the build-up of queues, and even measure table turnover times in restaurants.[6]
- Disney took a similar approach to understanding the customer journey around its resorts, but using wearable technology. Park guests are issued with a MagicBand wristband that acts as a ride pass, hotel room key, payment device and more. The band also communicates

with sensors as customers move around the resort, which means Disney knows exactly where customers are and what they're doing.[7] For example, when customers access a ride, data is sent in real time to the operations team, which can then make decisions about adding staff in certain areas of the park or incentivizing guests to try out a different attraction in another part of the park. This makes for more efficient use of the park.

Although there are many opportunities to boost your internal data, it's likely you'll need additional data to fulfil your goals – or it could be that you simply don't have the means to gather the right data internally. This is where external data (such as social media data, demographic data, weather data, etc) comes in. Let's explore the main options for accessing external data.

## Using publicly available data

This is external data that is freely available for people to use (as opposed to external data that is provided as a paid-for service – more on that coming up later). There are many fantastic options for accessing free, public data, including:

- The UK Data Service provides a number of datasets that can help you understand the needs of certain demographics.[8]
- Data.gov.uk is a great resource for market and consumer insights and includes data from central UK government, local authorities and public bodies.[9] For US government data check out Data.gov,[10] and for European public datasets there's the EU Open Data Portal.[11]
- World Bank Open Data provides datasets for population demographics and economic indicators from across the world.[12]
- Kaggle contains numerous open datasets, on anything from bike sharing in London to forest fires in Brazil.[13]
- Microsoft Research Open Data offers curated datasets from published research studies.[14]
- Amazon Web Services provides access to a wealth of public data, with easy searching and example use cases.[15]
- Google is working to make public data more discoverable through its Datasets Search Engine, which lets you search for datasets by name.[16]
- There's also Google Trends, which lets you analyse data on web search activity and trending topics from around the world.[17]

- For open image data, ImageNet contains millions of images across thousands of categories.[18] Alternatively, there's Google's Open Images Dataset.[19] For video data, there's YouTube 8M.[20]

The main disadvantage of using publicly available data is that, obviously, everyone can access it. Open data only tends to give you a competitive advantage if you can combine it in some unique way with other open or paid-for data, or use it with your own internal data. Another thing to be aware of is that access to public data could, in theory, be withdrawn at any time. In short, if the data you need is absolutely critical to your everyday business operations, I'd be very wary of relying solely on publicly available data.

### Buying external data

As well as freely available external data, there are plenty of providers that sell access to data. More and more companies are packaging and selling data, and I see this activity growing massively in the near future. For some companies, selling access to data provides an additional revenue stream – John Deere, which provides data-related add-on services for farmers (see Chapter 3) is a good example. Or gathering and selling data could be the company's main business activity – such companies are known as data brokers.

Data brokers have been around for decades, building databases on consumer activity for marketing or credit scoring purposes. But with the increasing datafication of our world, data brokers have adapted to hoover up far richer and more insight-laden streams of information. Some of the largest data brokers around are:

- Acxiom is a world leader in direct marketing data, particularly for data on US households.
- Nielsen is huge in market research, consumer behaviour and ratings data.
- Experian combines credit scoring with marketing expertise and offers its data services across a range of industries, not just finance.
- Equifax is another company that started out in credit scores, but now has data on more than 800 million consumers, almost 90 million businesses and employee data from more than 5,000 employers.

In addition to these data brokers, you can buy access to data from weather companies, satellite companies, telecoms businesses, credit card providers, and social media platforms – often via simple *application programming interfaces* (APIs, essentially a tool that allows two applications to talk to each other). Using APIs, developers can connect to and interrogate datasets. For example, the Weather2020 API provides predictive weather analytics with accurate long-range forecasts. A retailer, for example, could combine this weather data with internal sales data to predict demand for products more accurately and support planning decisions. In another example, social media companies like Twitter usually offer a range of premium APIs to help users interrogate their data.

## Crowdsourcing external data

Sometimes the data you need isn't easy to get hold of – the data may be out there in various different forms, but not packaged up in a neat, ready-made dataset for you to interrogate. Crowdsourcing data gives you a way to gather up external data when it isn't already available as a ready-made dataset. A great early example of this is the City of Boston, which created an app that allowed residents to report potholes in the road – making it much easier for the city to gather data on road conditions.

In the age of AI, gathering data is even easier, especially thanks to advances like machine vision. Non-profit organization Wild Me uses machine vision to combat wildlife extinction, by gathering sightings of wildlife from social media. Wild Me's AI can scroll social media and recognize animals in social media posts, pictures and videos. The AI can recognize animals from images, identify whether it has seen that particular animal before, and identify the animal's location. This provides an ingenious new way to monitor wildlife without putting trackers on them – and it's all thanks to the power of the crowd.

## Augmenting existing data

I mentioned earlier in the chapter that AI is likely to need less data in future, as machines become more intelligent and better at learning from small datasets. But, for now, the training of AI models still relies on huge datasets. So what do you do if your data just isn't big enough to train AI? Data augmentation provides a way to create more data and variations of data, from existing small datasets. This is great if you need to increase the diversity of a data training set for AI, without having to collect new data.

## Creating synthetic data

As well as augmenting existing real-life data, you can now create entirely synthetic data that can be used to train AI algorithms. Synthetic data is any data that's been artificially produced by a computer (as opposed to collected from a real-world situation) but is as close as possible to the properties of data from the real world.

This is useful in a number of ways. For one thing, it reduces the time, cost and risk involved in gathering real-life data. It can also provide a boost when there isn't enough real-life data to properly train an AI, or when real-life data can't be used for privacy reasons. Ultimately, synthetic data may help to democratize AI and open it up to companies that aren't creating masses of data on a daily basis. Research by MIT suggests it's possible to get the same results using synthetic data as you would with real data.[21]

Here's an example of synthetic data from the digital world being put to good use in the real world. A team at Princeton University used the video game Grand Theft Auto to help an AI learn about stop signs – how the signs look in different lights, how they look when they're covered in mud and snow, how they look when partially obscured, etc.[22] The AI can be used to help self-driving cars learn how to navigate on real-life roads. Similarly, Google's self-driving car unit Waymo tested its autonomous vehicles by driving 8 million miles on real roads and 5 billion miles on simulated roads.[23]

## Getting your data fit for use

You've gathered or accessed the data you need. Now what?

## Preparing your data properly

AI doesn't just need the right quantity of data; it also needs the right quality data – data that's been thoroughly prepared to ensure insights are accurate, consistent and lead to action. It's a bit like the cooking process. Preparing your raw ingredients is an essential step in creating a delicious meal, and the same is true of data and analytics. It's particularly true when your data comes from a variety of disparate sources (which it probably will). You can't just throw a load of different ingredients in a pot and hope something edible comes out at the end;

you need to ensure all ingredients are thoroughly prepped and will work together.

As every project is likely to be different and involve different data, there are no hard and fast checklists to follow here. You'll therefore need to devise a workflow that's unique to your data and AI project – just as you would check you have the right ingredients and that you know what to do with them before you start cooking. But as a general rule, you'll need to consider the following steps:

- **Data cleansing** – which means removing data that is inaccurate, damaged or corrupt, or identifying missing data. No dataset is perfect, but the quality of data affects the quality of the outcomes, so tidying up your data is a vital step. This should also include checking for biases in the data.
- **Metadata creation** – which essentially means labelling data to make it easier for an analytics system to know what to do with it.
- **Data transformation** – which involves putting data into the correct format for your analytics system to work with.
- **Data standardization** – which means making sure your data points are presented in a uniform way, such as all dates being in an eight-digit form rather than a six-digit form.
- **Data augmentation** – which I've already mentioned earlier in the chapter, can be used to extrapolate additional information based on what's already known.

Because AI is generally using lots of data, it's not usually possible to do all this manually. However, a large and growing market for data preparation tools has emerged, many of them requiring a minimum of data science knowledge.

## Considering ownership, ethics and privacy

You may not 'own' all the data you're using. You may, for example, be accessing external weather data or tapping into social media APIs. But as data becomes a source of competitive advantage, ownership becomes more and more important. For any data that's absolutely critical to core business operations, I'd always advise owning that data yourself wherever possible (which may mean you need to invest in new systems to gather that data, rather than relying on external sources). That's not to say external data isn't important – in fact, it can be an incredibly rich source of insights. Just don't overlook the fact that you don't own the data, and the terms of access to that data could change at any time.

As for ethics and privacy, those are topics I've already covered in detail in Chapter 9, so circle back there for a refresher on the main ethics considerations. A key point to remember here is, just because you own certain data or have access to certain data, that doesn't mean you have the right to use it for AI. You need to ensure you have the right consent in place for the intended use. Stakeholder trust is absolutely critical, so always be transparent on what data you're gathering and how you intend to use it.

### Protecting your data

Again, this is something I talked about in Chapter 9, so I won't repeat myself here. The main point I want to stress here is that data is both an asset and a liability, especially when it comes to personally identifiable data. Make sure you have the proper systems in place to securely store your data and keep it safe.

Homomorphic encryption is one cutting-edge area that offers great potential for AI systems to learn from data without seeing the data – as in, the data can remain encrypted, which is great for security, yet can still be used to train AIs.

### Keeping data up to date

You may have a great dataset, train your AI perfectly and have an analytics system that works brilliantly. But if you don't keep your data up to date, its usefulness will diminish pretty quickly. It's therefore important you keep systems updated, keep looking for gaps and inaccuracies in your datasets, and stay on the lookout for new datasets that can be added to your analytics.

---

**KEY TAKEAWAYS**

In this chapter we've learned:

- At present, AI systems need lots of data in order to learn. But the intelligent machines of the future are likely to be able to learn from more limited datasets, as they develop advanced reasoning that is more like human intelligence.

---

- Instead of attempting to collect data on everything, take a balanced approach to data. Prioritize data that will help deliver your strategic use cases (as identified in Chapter 7) but try to see data as an overall business asset that you want to grow.

- What type and how much data you need will depend on what you're trying to achieve and the complexity of the problem you're trying to solve.

- When it comes to finding the right data, start by auditing the data you already have. Then, where you need additional data, options for gathering data include: collecting new data yourself, using publicly available data, buying external data, crowdsourcing data, augmenting existing data, and creating synthetic data.

- Finally, you need to prepare your data for use, consider ownership and ethics issues, take steps to protect your data, and ensure you keep your data up to date.

Getting the right data in place is a critical hurdle to overcome on your AI journey, and one that will no doubt require something of a technology overhaul. In the next chapter, we delve into the technology side of AI.

## Endnotes

1   Hale, T (2017) How much data does the world generate every minute? *IFL Science*, https://www.iflscience.com/technology/how-much-data-does-the-world-generate-every-minute/ (archived at https://perma.cc/H5RC-PYQE)

2   Khvoynitskaya, S (2018) The future of big data: 5 predictions from experts, *itransition*, https://www.itransition.com/blog/the-future-of-big-data (archived at https://perma.cc/PW3C-UHMH)

3   Reinsel, D *et al* (2018) Data age 2025: the digitization of the world, *IDC*, https://www.seagate.com/files/www-content/our-story/trends/files/idc-seagate-dataage-whitepaper.pdf (archived at https://perma.cc/B9CL-73BU)

4   Statista (2019) A minute on the internet in 2019, https://www.statista.com/chart/17518/internet-use-one-minute/ (archived at https://perma.cc/8X5L-JY3D)

5   Withers, R (2018) The iPhone's face ID struggles in the morning, *Slate*, https://slate.com/technology/2018/07/iphone-face-id-struggles-to-recognize-people-in-the-morning.html?via=gdpr-consent (archived at https://perma.cc/AW56-WJ2V)

6   Marr, B (2019) AI on cruise ships: the fascinating ways Royal Caribbean uses facial recognition and machine vision, *Forbes*, https://www.forbes.com/sites/

bernardmarr/2019/05/10/the-fascinating-ways-royal-caribbean-uses-facial-recognition-and-machine-vision/#7f41e4b91524 (archived at https://perma.cc/HYK2-YLH3)

7    Marr, B (2017) Disney uses big data, IoT and machine learning to boost customer experience, *Forbes*, https://www.forbes.com/sites/bernardmarr/2017/08/24/disney-uses-big-data-iot-and-machine-learning-to-boost-customer-experience/#3e1ce65c3387 (archived at https://perma.cc/JM74-3QH8)

8    UK Data Service, https://www.ukdataservice.ac.uk/ (archived at https://perma.cc/HZN3-UP9E)

9    Find open data; https://data.gov.uk/ (archived at https://perma.cc/K36P-VQLZ)

10   Data.gov, https://www.data.gov/ (archived at https://perma.cc/AD64-SERS)

11   EU Open Data Portal, https://data.europa.eu/euodp/en/data/ (archived at https://perma.cc/QJ3L-6GTU)

12   World Bank Open Data, https://data.worldbank.org/ (archived at https://perma.cc/M8LD-T4C5)

13   Kaggle datasets, https://www.kaggle.com/datasets (archived at https://perma.cc/4YNK-MY5R)

14   Microsoft Research Open Data, https://msropendata.com/ (archived at https://perma.cc/525H-JKT5)

15   Open Data on AWS, https://aws.amazon.com/opendata/ (archived at https://perma.cc/SNQ2-6TRK)

16   Google Dataset Search, https://datasetsearch.research.google.com (archived at https://perma.cc/K4AM-UKNX)

17   Google Trends, https://trends.google.com/trends/?geo=US (archived at https://perma.cc/BGA4-NA2J)

18   ImageNet, http://www.image-net.org/ (archived at https://perma.cc/NKT8-MW8F)

19   Google Open Images Dataset, https://opensource.google/projects/open-images-dataset (archived at https://perma.cc/56YD-VCNJ)

20   YouTube 8M; https://research.google.com/youtube8m/ (archived at https://perma.cc/YT7Q-Z8J7)

21   Koperniak, S (2017) Artificial data give the same results as real data – without compromising privacy, *MIT News*, http://news.mit.edu/2017/artificial-data-give-same-results-as-real-data-0303 (archived at https://perma.cc/NJ3X-VUQL)

22   Marr, B (nd) Artificial intelligence: the clever ways video games are used to train AIs, https://www.bernardmarr.com/default.asp?contentID=1513 (archived at https://perma.cc/N5KW-J9XL)

23   Hawkins, A (2018) Waymo's autonomous cars have driven 8 million miles on public roads, *The Verge*, https://www.theverge.com/2018/7/20/17595968/waymo-self-driving-cars-8-million-miles-testing (archived at https://perma.cc/EP6Y-8H2F)

# CHAPTER ELEVEN

# The need for a technology overhaul

A I requires certain technology – the technology to store data and run AI processes, for example. Getting this right can be a huge challenge, particularly for established businesses that invested heavily in technology maybe 10 years ago. Today, such businesses are finding that technology that was right for the previous industrial revolution is no longer right for the intelligence revolution. Technology moves on. As a result, these businesses risk being overtaken by new startups – digital-native organizations – that aren't hampered by legacy technology systems holding them back (a good example being the rash of fintech startups that are challenging established banks).

Therefore, to fully embrace the AI revolution, you may need to rethink your technology infrastructure. Thankfully, there are many solutions out there to choose from. In this chapter, however, I'll try to avoid going into too much detail on individual solutions – precisely because the technology moves on so quickly. Instead, we'll focus on the factors to consider when reviewing your technology needs, and look at solutions for companies that don't necessarily have the in-house skills and knowledge required to develop an AI infrastructure from scratch.

## Linking technology needs to the four layers of AI and data

There's an awful lot of behind-the-scenes technology that goes into making machines intelligent. Behind the exciting examples of AI in action that we've seen throughout this book, there are data collection systems, vast data warehouses, computer processing units crunching through masses of data, and innovative reporting tools that help humans collaborate with intelligent machines. Broadly speaking, the technology that goes into today's cutting-edge AI can be broken down into four processes or layers that make up the AI technology stack. These layers are:

- data collection;
- data storage;
- data processing and analytics;
- data output and reporting.

Let's look at each layer in turn.

### Data collection

As we saw in Chapter 10, AI is dependent on the data that is gathered. Therefore, for this layer, you must think about the technology you'll need to have in place to collect data. This data may come from a number of places. From industrial machinery to the smart phones we carry everywhere we go, smart IoT devices and sensors have given businesses many exciting new ways to collect data. The data collection layer of an AI stack is composed of software that interfaces with these smart devices, but it may also include web-based services that supply third-party data, such as marketing databases or weather and social media APIs (see Chapter 10). Remember, this data can come in many forms these days, including natural human language, activity data, image data and more.

### Data storage

Once you've collected data, or set up access to third-party data feeds, you need somewhere to put that data. Because AI data is usually Big Data (see Chapter 2), it needs a lot of storage space, and it needs to be storage that can be accessed quickly and easily.

Thanks to advances in computing power, data storage is becoming a lot cheaper, and we now have the ability to store almost unlimited amounts of data (which is a good thing when you consider we're doubling the amount of data generated every two years). Some businesses have the capability and resources to establish their own data centres or data lakes, using technology such as Hadoop or Spark, to cope with the vast amount of information being generated. But for many businesses, this just isn't possible. This is where cloud storage has come into its own. Third-party cloud infrastructure – such as Amazon Web Services – provides a workable solution for many businesses, since storage can be scaled up or down when needed. These platforms tend to integrate easily with analytics and output services (see the next two layers), which is another advantage for businesses looking to get the most out of data and AI.

What you'll need to think about for this layer is whether you want to completely outsource your data storage to an off-the-peg cloud storage solution, or create your own private infrastructure where you're completely in control. Or you may opt for a hybrid solution, where certain datasets are kept in-house, while others are outsourced to external cloud providers.

## Data processing and analytics

Though all four layers are vital for generating valuable insights, this layer is the one that people tend to focus on when they talk about AI technology. AI processing is the meaty part, essentially, where algorithms work to make sense of data. This analytics process may encompass machine learning, deep learning, image recognition, natural language processing, sentiment analysis, recommendation engines – and other tech buzzwords we've explored throughout this book.

As we've already seen in this book, it's the self-learning capabilities of AI algorithms that really differentiates the current wave of AI from what has come before – together with the increase in the amount of data available. But that all requires a lot of raw processing power. Today the increase in available processing power comes from the deployment of graphics processing units, or GPUs – processors originally designed for the very heavy-duty task of generating sophisticated computer visuals. Their mathematical prowess makes them ideal for repurposing as data-crunchers. A new wave of processing units specifically designed for handling AI-related tasks should provide a further leap in AI performance in the future, particularly if advances like quantum computing (see Chapter 2) take off.

AI algorithms are often provided in the form of services which are either accessed through a third-party API, deployed on a public cloud, or run in a private data centre, data lake or, in the case of edge analytics, at the point of data collection itself (for example, within sensor or data capture hardware). AI-as-a-service means businesses don't necessarily need to build this technology for themselves – you can tap into ready-made AI tools and 'plug in' your data. (Although, for very complex or highly strategic goals, you may want or need to develop your own AI algorithms.) There's more on AI-as-a-service coming up later in the chapter.

## Data output and reporting

Your technology requirements for data output will depend on what you're trying to achieve. For example, if the aim of your AI strategy is to get machines working more efficiently and effectively together (perhaps for predictive maintenance purposes, to minimize resource usage, or to streamline or automate business processes) then this layer will encompass technology that communicates the insights from your AI processing systems to the relevant business systems or machinery that need those insights. So, if you have an automated tool that assesses mortgage applicants and gives them a decision in minutes, then the AI analytics technology will need to communicate with whatever system acts as the customer interface.

Alternatively, if your goal is to enable better decision making within the business, you'll need technology that can communicate insights for team members to take action on. One example of this might be sales assistants using handheld terminals to read insights and recommendations relating to customers who are standing in front of them. In some cases, the output may be in the form of charts, graphics and dashboards. However, voice interfaces – think of technology such as Siri and Cortana – can also play a role here, as they make data output more intuitive and digestible. In my experience, the combination of visuals and natural language can make insights much easier to understand and act upon.

Ultimately, there are many different outputs that can be generated by AI systems, and there are no hard and fast rules to follow. What's right for your business will depend upon what you're trying to achieve and who or what needs to act upon the insights generated by AI.

## Taking into account your industry-specific needs

While the four layers of the AI tech stack serve as a useful starting point, keep in mind it's a framework only. There will no doubt be other factors to consider that are specific to your industry. For example, there may be certain regulations that restrict how you can store or process data, and these will need to be considered alongside the four layers.

Or there may be competitive considerations that affect your technology infrastructure decisions. For example, the recently launched Amazon Forecast tool is a great example of a third-party machine learning tool that businesses can use without creating their own technology.[1] Available in certain regions through the Amazon Web Service platform, and based on Amazon's own forecasting engine, the tool helps retailers predict demand for products. Sounds great, right? Absolutely. But retailers – who may count Amazon as a key rival – may not want to use an Amazon service to help boost internal performance. And yet the tool could be a great resource for smaller retailers who don't have access to in-house data scientists...

Ultimately, when considering your AI technology needs, you'll need to find that sweet spot between leveraging externally available tools and maintaining control over your own data, processes and sources of competitive advantage.

## A (brief) look at hardware requirements for AI

Many people focus on the software requirements for AI, but it's important not to overlook hardware requirements. Nowadays, there's more hardware available that is specifically customized for AI – one example being AI-optimized chips in mobile phones.

### Say goodbye to Moore's Law

Back in 1965, Gordon Moore, co-founder of Intel, observed that the number of transistors on a square inch on integrated circuits doubled every year, meaning a doubling of computing power. In 1975, he revised that to every two years. This insight became known as Moore's Law. In practice, this means transistors have got smaller (meaning computer manufacturers could fit more of them in a smaller space, thus increasing memory space), processing power has increased, computers have got smaller, and computing power is now much more economically viable. This dramatic, exponential boost to computing power has changed the way we work and live forever.

Moore's prediction ended up proving accurate for decades. Only in 2015 did Intel announce that the pace of acceleration had slowed to a point where it was doubling approximately every two and a half years.[2] In effect, chip manufacturing has reached such tiny scales that there's a limit to how much further they can be miniaturized. We'll struggle to make smaller transistors, in other words, which means Moore's Law no longer holds true. Computing power is slowing down.

### What's next after GPUs?

The demise of Moore's Law is interesting from an AI perspective because AI is an insatiable compute-hungry beast. How will hardware keep pace with AI demands when it's no longer accelerating at the pace it was? GPUs have, so far, dominated in the field of AI hardware. But as demand for AI increases, GPU systems may not be able to keep up. New, specially designed AI hardware will have to be created.

Researchers are racing to develop various solutions to this, including neuromorphic computing (using electronic circuits to mimic the neuro-biological architectures of the nervous system), optical computing (replacing electrons with photons), customized AI chips (for example, chips in mobile phones which allow some of the analytics to be done on the device), quantum computing (unimaginably fast computers) and biological computing (using biologically derived molecules, such as DNA, to store and process data).

Companies such as Intel, Microsoft, Nvidia and Google are working hard to develop the AI hardware of the future. Ultimately, thanks to the demise of Moore's Law and the ever-increasing demands of AI, the supercomputing hardware of the future may be very different from the traditional hardware we see today.

### Tapping into AI-as-a-service

Today, companies of all kinds are used to tapping into as-a-service offerings, particularly when it comes to software. Rather than purchasing software as a one-off cost, many companies nowadays will access software on a subscription/platform model – paying a monthly or annual fee to remotely access software through a cloud-based platform. The same sort of thing is possible for AI solutions, hence the name AI-as-a-service.

## What is AI-as-a-service (AIaaS)?

I briefly touched on AIaaS in Chapters 5 and 8, but because AIaaS is a key option for many businesses embarking on their AI journey, it makes sense to delve into it in more detail.

As you've probably guessed already, AI technology isn't cheap. Building and testing the machine learning algorithms and putting in place the right hardware can be prohibitively expensive, which is why AI has so far largely been the domain of tech giants such as Google and Amazon. For companies who can't, or don't want to, build everything from scratch, AIaaS is a great solution.

Think of AIaaS as an off-the-shelf AI technology offering, where you tap into third-party, ready-made AI tools, without having to invest in expensive infrastructure or new hires. (Although you may not need to hire in new skills, it is absolutely still worth investing in data and AI training for your teams, in order to raise data literacy across the organization. See Chapter 8.) These AIaaS solutions lower the barriers to entry, opening AI up to a wider range of businesses, including very small businesses. Thanks to AIaaS, pretty much any company can use AI to create smarter products, more intelligent services and enhanced business processes, without spending mega-bucks. If you have the data – or you can access the data you need through other sources, see Chapter 10 – AIaaS means you can begin using AI almost immediately.

I'll get to some examples of AIaaS platforms later, but typical examples of AIaaS tools include:

- **Chatbots and digital assistants**
  These are currently the most widely used AIaaS tool, particularly for customer service.
- **APIs (application programming interfaces)**
  These allow developers to plug off-the-peg technology into applications without having to create all the code themselves. An example might be plugging a weather data tool into a business forecasting application.

- **Machine learning frameworks and services**
  There's a wide range of sophisticated offerings that can be applied to more complex AI tasks. These solutions can range from customizable pre-built frameworks and models that you can adapt to your own needs, or fully managed machine learning services.

## The pros and cons of AIaaS

Starting with the positives, the main benefits of AIaaS include:

- **Lower costs**
  With AIaaS you can avoid the initial investment and ongoing maintenance of AI software and hardware, not to mention the costs of hiring developers and data scientists. What's more, AIaaS costs are transparent, and with many offerings you only pay for what you use.
- **Flexibility and scalability**
  You can scale up and down easily, adapting your AI use to suit your changing business needs. For example, you can start by applying AI in one area of the business, and then expand from there.
- **User friendliness**
  With many off-the-shelf AIaaS solutions, you don't need to become an AI expert in order to use the tool.

And the downsides?

- **Data security**
  If you're using your own data for AI, you'll obviously need to share that data with the third-party AIaaS vendor. You'll need to make sure the transfer of data is secure and that the vendor has robust data security processes in place. Also, be aware of any data security and privacy rules that may limit your ability to use AIaaS. (More on data security, privacy and ethics in Chapter 9.)
- **Ongoing costs**
  Yes, you won't have that initial investment, but you will have the ongoing AIaaS fees to budget for. It can be tempting to quickly start plugging these solutions into multiple areas of the business, which means costs may shoot up quickly, so keep your AI use targeted and strategic to ensure the costs (and outcomes) remain on-course. Circle back to Chapter 7 for more on developing an AI strategy.

- **The 'black box' problem**
  As we saw in Chapter 9, it's not always clear how AI does what it does. How explainable is your AIaaS offering – how does it arrive at its outcomes?
- **Dependence on a third party**
  When you develop solutions in-house, you're in control. By opting for an AIaaS offering, you're effectively reliant on another company to deliver your AI goals. What happens if your AIaaS vendor cuts you off? (Unlikely, but even so.) Or what happens if there's an outage of the service?

Only you can weigh up these pros and cons and decide whether AIaaS is right for you. For example, if what you're using AI for is absolutely vital to the successful everyday operation of the company, and a key part of your competitive advantage, you may want to consider building your own in-house solution. Or, you may get started with an AIaaS solution then, as your AI activities grow, you may decide to bring those functions in-house. Or you may decide the ease and simplicity of AIaaS hugely outweighs any downsides for your organization.

### Who offers AIaaS?

At the time of writing, some of the biggest AIaaS providers are the household names you'd expect: Amazon, Google, IBM and Microsoft. Most of them offer the full range of AIaaS tools, from simple chatbots to fully managed machine learning services. Let's take a brief look at each one in turn.

#### AMAZON WEB SERVICES (AWS)

Amazon's cloud computing platform houses a number of AI tools, including Amazon Forecast, which I mentioned earlier in the chapter. Another machine learning-based service on AWS is Amazon Personalize, which companies can use to develop websites, apps and other solutions that provide personalized recommendations for customers – think tailored search results, or product recommendations based on customer activity (page views, purchases, clicks, etc.). At the time of writing, Personalize was only available in certain locations, but more locations will be added.[3]

### GOOGLE CLOUD

Google's platform features a wide range of 'plug-and-play' machine learning products, designed to encourage experimentation and help developers bring machine learning projects to life. Google also has TensorFlow, which is an open source software library for building machine learning tools.

### IBM WATSON DEVELOPER CLOUD

Through this platform companies can deploy IBM's Watson intelligence in their applications, and seamlessly embed AI in organizational work-flows. The suite of options available includes Watson Assistant chatbot and virtual assistant technology, which lets you build conversational interfaces into applications and devices.

### MICROSOFT AZURE

Microsoft offers a wide range of cloud services via Azure, allowing companies to build, manage and deploy various applications using ready-made tools and frameworks. Its tools have been deployed across industries such as healthcare, banking, retail and manufacturing.

### OTHER PROVIDERS

Outside of the household name tech giants like Amazon and Microsoft, there are vendors that specialize in AI for specific fields. For example, Salesforce, which is known for its customer relationship management software, has an AI tool called Einstein which allows companies to apply AI to their customer data.

China and India are also gunning to be leaders in AI, and you'll find impressive cloud computing platforms from both Chinese and Indian technology companies. Chinese conglomerate Alibaba, for instance, offers Alibaba Cloud, which provides machine learning services such as model training, model prediction and data processing. And Chinese internet giant Tencent has its AI Open Platform, which allows businesses to harness the power of Tencent's AI Lab. Out of India, Wipro has its HOLMES AI and automation platform.

### AIaaS in action: how two companies turned to AIaaS to solve their business problems

To show what's possible, let's look at a couple of real-world examples of companies tapping into AIaaS platforms.

Bradesco, one of Brazil's largest banks with 65 million customers, turned to IBM Watson to help answer customer queries faster and provide a better, more personalized service. Previously, when branch staff had a question about services or products, they'd have to call the bank's central office, which often created long delays for customers who were waiting for answers. In an industry where fintech startups are challenging incumbent organizations for customers, particularly digitally native customers, this clunky way of doing things couldn't last.

So Bradesco turned to Watson to get faster answers. But first, Watson had to learn Portuguese and learn about the company's banking products and processes. After training on 10,000 queries – across 62 different products – Watson was tested in a limited number of branches before being rolled out and made available to all 5,200 branches across Brazil. Instead of having to call head office and wait for answers, branch staff simply ask Watson (in writing or via spoken query) and get a response within seconds. Watson now answers 283,000 product questions a month, with 95 per cent accuracy, meaning just 5 per cent of queries need further assistance.[4] Employees are now able to answer customer queries in-branch much faster, and devote more time to delivering great service.

Elsewhere, Wipro's AI platform HOLMES helped a leading Australasian insurer detect 98 per cent of fraud claims – achieving a 40 times improvement over the company's previous fraud detection system. In particular, a high number of false positives meant a lot of time was being spent investigating non-fraudulent cases, delaying insurance payments for genuine customers.

Thanks to its self-learning algorithms and ability to understand patterns, HOLMES was able to improve the company's fraud detection rule-based models, improve accuracy in assessing insurance claims, and accurately predict fraud claims.[5]

## Three ways to get the most out of AIaaS

AIaaS provides a great way to get up and running with AI relatively quickly, without the potentially huge expense of developing models and infrastructure yourself. But, as you will have seen from the list of pros and cons, AIaaS isn't without its challenges. Here are three tips to help you get the most out of AIaaS:

- **Teach teams about AI and data**

  You don't need everyone to be data scientists and AI experts, but you do need people to be aware of the benefits of AI, why the company is turning to AIaaS, and how AIaaS can help drive business improvements. Teams will need specific training on how to use the AIaaS system, but I also recommend implementing a data literacy training programming. (Circle back to Chapter 8 for more on raising data literacy and other people-related concerns.)

- **Start small and build from there**

  It's important to be realistic and recognize that AI isn't going to transform your business overnight. Trying to adopt AI in too many different areas of the business at once is unlikely to prove successful. Therefore, I recommend starting small, with just a small number of key AI use cases (see Chapter 7), and expanding gradually from there.

- **Measure results (and shout successes from the rooftops)**

  As with any new technology, you need to know it's working for you and delivering the results you need. Based on your strategic goals (see Chapter 7), I recommend putting in place a reporting system of KPIs that will help you assess the impact of AIaaS. And when AI has boosted business performance, be sure to communicate that across the business – it'll help promote buy-in for future AI projects.

---

KEY TAKEAWAYS

In this chapter we've learned:

- When considering your technology needs, it helps to consider the four layers of the AI technology stack: data collection, data storage, data processing and analytics, and data output and reporting. You'll also need to take into account other factors that are specific to your industry or region, such as regulations that restrict how you can store data.

- Be sure to consider both hardware and software requirements. Today, more hardware is being specifically designed to cope with compute-heavy AI processes, and researchers are racing to develop supercomputing hardware better able to cope with increasing demand for AI.

- AI-as-a-service (AIaaS) is opening up AI to a far wider range of companies. There are pros and cons to weigh up but, in general, AIaaS is a great option for businesses who don't want to or can't build their AI solutions from scratch.

As well as technology challenges, AI poses a number of leadership challenges, from securing buy-in for AI approaches, to managing organizational change (including increasing automation). Read more about these leadership considerations in the next chapter.

## Endnotes

1  ResearchLive (2019) Amazon forecast tool launched, https://www.research-live.com/article/news/amazon-forecast-tool-launched/id/5058012 (archived at https://perma.cc/7HR5-JGPS)

2  Bradshaw, T (2015) Intel chief raises doubts over Moore's Law, *Financial Times*, https://www.ft.com/content/36b722bc-2b49-11e5-8613-e7aedbb7bdb7 (archived at https://perma.cc/4JWM-T59M)

3  Wiggers, K (2019) Amazon launches Personalize, a fully managed AI-powered recommendation service, *VentureBeat*, https://venturebeat.com/2019/06/10/amazon-launches-personalize-a-fully-managed-ai-powered-recommendation-service/ (archived at https://perma.cc/S7EU-U4Q6)

4  Morris, E (nd) How a Brazilian bank pays personal attention to each of their 65 million customers, *IBM Watson*, https://www.ibm.com/watson/stories/bradesco/ (archived at https://perma.cc/QE2V-33HE)

5  Wipro (nd) Wipro HOLMES helps insurer detect 98% of fraud claims, https://www.wipro.com/holmes/holmes-helps-insurer-detect-98--of-fraud-claims-/ (archived at https://perma.cc/BE7W-GEAS)

# CHAPTER TWELVE

# Leadership challenges in the intelligence revolution

As we saw in Chapter 8, the workplace is changing. The organizations of the future will have flatter hierarchies, business boundaries will become more porous, constant innovation will be the norm, workplaces will become decentralized, partnerships will become more important, and there will be more gig jobs. It makes sense, then, that business leaders in this intelligence revolution will need to adapt. The way we run businesses will change, and the people running them will need a different set of skills.

In a sense, this entire book is about the leadership challenges brought about by the intelligence revolution; working out how to use AI, dealing with people-related challenges, avoiding the ethical pitfalls of AI, making sure you have the right technology in place, and so on – all are key considerations for the business leaders of today and tomorrow. My goal in this chapter is not to repeat or condense those challenges – more, it's to look at what all these challenges mean for being a good leader in the intelligence revolution.

First and foremost, a good leader doesn't ignore the intelligence revolution, or allow other leaders in their organization to ignore it. (Therefore, reading this book is a great first step!) In my experience, there's a yawning gap developing between those companies where the leadership boards are acutely aware of the dramatic changes coming their way, and those companies with leaders who are (sometimes wilfully) ignorant of the impact of data and AI on their industry. Leaders in the second camp, who cling to the status quo, will find themselves outpaced and outdated in a very short space of time.

## It's your role to approach AI strategically

I spend a lot of time talking to senior leadership teams, helping them understand the AI revolution, and a common worry among leaders is they don't have a deep enough understanding of the finer technical details of AI. My response is this: while you do need a certain level of understanding – particularly when it comes to the wider impact of AI and how it can be used – you don't need to be a tech genius to be a good leader in the intelligence revolution. It's your job to ensure the technology is applied in a strategic way.

### Taking a strategic view of AI

As we saw in Chapter 7, this means identifying how best to use AI in your business – whether that means creating smarter products, smarter services, smarter business processes, or a combination of the three. What specific business challenges can AI and data help solve? How can AI and data drive success in the business? It's your role to ask these questions and make sure AI is implemented in a way that best benefits the business.

It's also your role to continually reflect on and review the strategic use of AI. This may include:

• finding new business strategies that take advantage of AI;
• identifying new applications of AI;
• reimagining business models as the intelligence revolution unfolds.

In my view, this process of reflection must take place continually, not as part of an annual review. (This is in addition to formally revising and updating your AI strategy, as described in Chapter 7.) In other words, as a leader, AI isn't something you 'do' and then forget about.

### Ensuring AI has a strategic sponsor in the business

Every leader should have a decent understanding of the intelligence revolution, but it's also wise to make sure AI has a strategic sponsor in the company. This is where the role of 'chief intelligence officer' can be very valuable. Ideally, this role isn't siloed into a specific business unit, and is entirely separate from the role of chief data officer.

The chief intelligence officer (or chief AI officer) should act as a bridge between the AI/data teams, the leadership team and the business teams, supporting AI strategy and implementation. This will likely include:

- helping to set the overarching vision for using AI;
- educating people across the company on the importance of AI;
- putting in place the frameworks needed to use AI in an ethical, responsible way;
- building the right skills, capacity and technology infrastructure;
- overseeing execution and delivery;
- managing stakeholders throughout this process.

We can expect this role to gain greater prominence over the next couple of years, prompting organizations across all industries to consider creating their own CIO role.

## Leading people through the changes

Beyond making sure AI is approached strategically, successful leaders in the intelligence revolution will be adept at managing AI execution and change.

### Making AI work in your organization – focusing on deployment, not development

In my experience, many businesses struggle to implement AI on any real scale. That's because businesses spend far too long on *development* – an approach that worked perfectly well in the previous industrial revolutions, but is no longer suitable in the fast-moving intelligence revolution. If you spend years developing, for example, an AI-enhanced version of your product, it'll be out of date by the time of its release. AI is forever changing the pace of business, which means *deployment*, not development, must be your watchword. This means focusing on rolling out AI (in a strategic way, of course), making it work, delivering real business benefits, failing fast when you fail, and learning quickly from mistakes.

So, although you may start applying AI in one part of the business (as opposed to trying to implement AI across the whole business at once), that doesn't mean you can afford to stand still. You will have to find ways to scale up your AI deployment, build upon your successes in other parts of the business, and learn from things that haven't quite gone to plan. This process must happen continually if you're to successfully scale up your AI activities.

### Remember, people will remain your most important asset

As a leader, your most important job is to lead people. The intelligence revolution doesn't change that. AI will have a profound impact on the workforce and will change the nature of work for many people the world over. It's vital that leaders address this head-on, by:

- **Focusing on people, rather than the technology**
  Even in the intelligence revolution, leaders can't afford to forget that people are still – and will remain – the business's most important asset. Good leaders will never lose sight of the ways in which humans add value (through creativity, problem solving, empathy, and so on).
- **Engaging with people about the importance of AI and data**
  Everyone in the organization must understand that AI is a business priority, and that data is what fuels AI. Therefore, data is a strategic business asset. Protecting and using data effectively and ethically is everyone's responsibility in the intelligence revolution. Good leaders will model this message every day.
- **Having continuous conversations about the impact of AI on the work of people**
  Good leaders won't attempt to gloss over or downplay the impact of AI, but will hold intelligent, open conversations with the workforce about the changes that are coming their way.
- **Actively bringing people along with them on the organization's AI journey**
  Good leaders will secure buy-in for AI across the business and ensure everyone understands how AI benefits the company, its customers, and its employees.

- **Embracing human–machine collaboration**
  All businesses will need to find the sweet spot between which roles/functions are best suited to humans and which are best suited to machines. Good leaders in the intelligence revolution will understand how to adapt workflows to get the best out of both humans and machines.
- **Investing in training and development**
  Good leaders will prepare their people for this new reality and ensure they have the skills they need in the intelligence revolution. This includes raising people's data literacy, helping them acquire new technical skills, and facilitating the development of critical soft skills.

### Depersonalizing decision making

You may have heard of the HiPPO (highest-paid person's opinion) effect, whereby teams defer to the opinion of the highest-paid person in the room when making decisions, rather than relying on hard data and evidence. And once the HiPPO has spoken, others may fear challenging their viewpoint or providing an alternative way forward.

Even with the advance of big data, the HiPPO effect is still very real in some organizations. Yet, in this intelligence revolution – with the sheer quantity and quality of data available today and the predictive capabilities of machines – deferring to the HiPPO in the room is just poor business practice. Thankfully, data and AI will help to democratize and depersonalize decision making in organizations. Although there will always be a place for instinct, intuition and experience, in the intelligence revolution decisions will be based largely on what the data says.

Therefore, good leaders will look for the data that supports decision making. But this doesn't mean blindly following data at the expense of critical thinking (see automation bias and the black box problem, Chapter 9). Leaders should invite disagreement, encourage people to challenge accepted wisdom, urge them to question the data that decisions are based upon, and build a workforce that thinks critically about how AI systems reach decisions.

## What do the successful leaders of the future look like?

I've mentioned several times throughout this book how uniquely human skills like creativity will become arguably more important in the age of

AI. So too will the role of human leadership skills. But it's highly likely that the successful leaders of the future will have a slightly different skillset from the traditional leadership skillset.

I believe successful leaders in the intelligence revolution will need to cultivate the following skills:

- **Agility**
  Leaders will have to be able to embrace and celebrate change, and view change not as a burden, but as an opportunity to grow and innovate. This includes embracing new technologies.
- **Emotional intelligence**
  Because, if we expect the workplaces of the future to prioritize human skills like emotional intelligence and empathy, it stands to reason that leaders must model these behaviours.
- **Cultural intelligence**
  The workplaces of the future will be even more diverse and global than they are today. Effective leaders will be able to appreciate and leverage the differences individuals bring to the table.
- **Humility (or, a balance between humility and confidence)**
  The leaders of the intelligence revolution will see themselves as facilitators and collaborators, rather than critical cogs to success. They'll encourage others to shine, in other words.
- **Accountability**
  As workplaces become more transparent and collaborative (through flatter organizational structures, partnership working, and so on), leaders will need to be more transparent and hold themselves accountable. Their actions must be in clear alignment with the company's goals.
- **Vision**
  Leaders in the intelligence revolution will need that big-picture vision in order to understand the impact of AI on the business and all of its stakeholders. Bearing this in mind, it's then up to leaders to determine how to meet all stakeholders' needs effectively.
- **Courage**
  We've barely scratched the surface of what AI can do so leaders will require the courage to face the unknown, the courage to fail fast, and the courage to change course when the situation calls for a new strategy. As part of this, they'll need the courage to identify their own weaknesses and be open to coaching and learning.

- **Intuition**
  Yes, data-driven decision making is the way forward, but leaders will still require that uniquely human skill of intuition, of being able to 'read' what's not being said.
- **Authenticity**
  Leaders in the intelligence revolution will need to be able to build trust, especially in times of uncertainty, change or failure. This requires leaders to exude authenticity.
- **Focus**
  Finally, with the incredible pace of change, and the continual need to adapt, future leaders will need to maintain a laser-like focus on the organization's objectives. They'll need to be able to cut through the chaos and hype to identify what's really important.

---

KEY TAKEAWAYS

In this chapter we've learned:

- The intelligence revolution brings with it many challenges that will change what it means to be a good leader. Its vital leaders don't ignore the intelligence revolution or allow other leaders in the organization to ignore it.
- Leaders must ensure AI is approached in a strategic way that helps the organization deliver its core business objectives. This will require leaders to continually reflect on and review the use of AI in the business.
- Consider introducing the role of chief intelligence officer to act as a strategic champion for AI within the business.
- To successfully implement AI, leaders will need to:
  - Focus on *deployment*, not development.
  - Remember that people are the most important asset for any business.
  - Watch out for the HiPPO effect. Decisions must be depersonalized and based on data.
- Human leadership skills will be just as important in the intelligence revolution, if not more so. But what we prize as key leadership skills in the future may look very different to traditional leadership skills. Softer, more human skills like humility, authenticity and emotional intelligence will become much more important.

---

Looking at the leaders of tomorrow brings us nicely to the final chapter of this book, where I take a glimpse into the future and look at how AI can help us overcome mankind's biggest challenges.

# CHAPTER THIRTEEN

# A look ahead

We're only at the beginning of this intelligence revolution. Progress is rapid, and astonishing breakthroughs are happening every year. Things that I thought I'd never see in my lifetime have been achieved in the last few years – and I say that as someone who works in the field of technology. This is not just the result of AI, of course. AI is part of a 'perfect storm' of technology trends, where AI is both driving other digital innovations and being influenced by them.[1] (Take the link between AI and the Internet of Things, for example, where each is driving rapid advances in the other.) As a result of this perfect storm of innovation, we can't yet imagine all the ways in which AI will impact our lives.

What we do know is that, in time, AI will become something we're all used to – just as we've seamlessly woven advances like the internet and mobile devices into our everyday lives. There will come a time, I'm sure, when younger generations can't believe people ever grew up without intelligent machines! As we look ahead to that time, what sort of future do we want to see: one where the intelligence revolution has positively transformed our world, or one in which AI is used in no end of creepy, underhand ways? Looking ahead, it is our responsibility to use the intelligence revolution to build the kind of world we all want to live in. I believe businesses have a vital role to play in this.

## Is AI the biggest opportunity we've ever had?

The intelligence revolution gives us an enormous opportunity to make our world a better place and address some of our most pressing challenges. It may even be the biggest opportunity we've ever had. But, on the flip side, there's huge scope to exploit and misuse the technology.

Businesses are pushing the boundaries of AI, so it's up to businesses to lead the way in the responsible use of AI. Leaders of organizations must examine their conscience here. Do we really just want to use this incredible technology to sell more things and make more money? Why not use AI to address those issues that really matter to stakeholders? To add real value to customers' lives, to make employees' working lives better, to solve problems, to deliver positive outcomes, and so on. (Happily, all are factors that help to make a business more valuable.)

Where businesses lead, I hope governments will follow. Because it's inevitable that AI will become increasingly political. Like businesses, governments have the opportunity to use AI to improve the lives of those they serve, or to control them.

As AI becomes adopted across wider society, it's vital people can trust the technology. Partly, this trust will be aided by greater regulation, data protection and increasing transparency on how AI systems reach decisions. But a big part of trusting AI comes down to how it's used by the organizations we interact with on a daily basis (governmental and private organizations). That includes transparency on what data is being collected, how that data is used, whether the data is biased, and so on. If we don't want to build a future in which AI is seen as a dark, nefarious and shadowy force, everything we do with AI *right now* matters.

## AI as a force for good

Perhaps it sounds like wishful thinking, this vision of a future in which AI helps us solve some of mankind's biggest problems. It shouldn't. In fact, there are plenty of examples of AI being used as a force for good:

- **Addressing climate change**
  From creating more intelligent, energy-efficient buildings to monitoring environmental issues like deforestation, AI can be deployed in a number of ways to help address climate change. In one example,

researchers from the Montreal Institute for Learning Algorithms, working with Microsoft and ConscientAI, have created an AI tool that simulates the impact of rising sea levels and more intense storms on people's homes. They plan to release an app that will show people what their homes and communities might look like in future, according to different climate change outcomes.[2]

- **Eliminating hunger**

  With an ever-increasing population, it's clear we need to become smarter and better at producing food. The LettuceBot from Blue River Technology can help growers apply herbicides more efficiently, so they only kill weeds and not crops. Having learned from pictures of 5,000 young plants, the system is able to tell the difference between weeds and young plants. When it identifies a weed, it sprays it directly, without contaminating other nearby plants, helping to cut plant losses by up to 90 per cent.[3]

- **Eradicating inequality and discrimination**

  AI is being put to use in a number of innovative ways to increase equal opportunities. Google's Lookout app, for instance, helps the visually impaired to identify objects in their surroundings. In another example, the Textio AI tool helps recruiters create more inclusive job descriptions. Software company Atlassian used the tool and managed to go from just 10 per cent female technical graduates to 57 per cent in two years.[4]

- **Overcoming illiteracy**

  With the clear link between poverty and illiteracy, overcoming illiteracy is a huge challenge for society. IBM has developed an app called Simpler Voice, which uses Watson's natural language processing capabilities to turn text into simple verbal messages.[5] From public signs to textbooks, the app is helping adults and children with low levels of literacy access and understand information. In another great example, Huawei has developed the StorySign app that helps deaf children learn to read by translating text from books into sign language. The mobile phone app is available for free.

- **Stopping the spread of disinformation and fake news**

  I talked a lot about fake content in Chapter 9 and it's clear that, while AI has enabled people to create worryingly convincing fakes, it's also the best weapon we have to combat the problem. In one example, the Fake News Challenge is exploring how AI can be used to automatically determine whether news is real or a hoax.[6]

- **Building resilience**
  There are several projects exploring how AI can be used to make infrastructure and communities more resilient in the face of disasters. For instance, a team from the University of Southern California's Center for Artificial Intelligence in Society is working with LA city officials to find technology solutions for aging, vulnerable water pipes. Their goal? To identify and carry out improvements to the most strategic pipelines so that, in the event of an earthquake, the water keeps flowing.[7]

## Some big changes will be needed

As you can probably tell, this is an area of AI that I get particularly excited about: using AI to create a future where everyone can reach their full potential. My kids, your kids, everybody's kids.

Building that world won't be easy. There will be sacrifices and challenges, and some profound changes will need to take place. Take the automation of human jobs as an example. Of course this is an emotive, concerning issue. But, if we're really honest with ourselves, are easily automated jobs really the sorts of jobs we should be allocating to humans? If we're going to create a fairer, more sustainable future, surely we don't want a world in which some humans are doing repetitive, mundane, perhaps even dangerous work – work that could be given to machines? If building a brighter future means replacing some human jobs, that's one of the changes we'll have to navigate.

AI has the potential to free us up from the less engaging things we do at work, giving us precious time back to do more of the things that matter to us. More time to spend with our children, to care for aging parents, to enjoy art and hobbies, to engage with our communities… all those things we want to do but never have the time for.

Perhaps we'll need to rethink the very nature of work for this to happen. For example, many companies are starting to embrace the notion of the four-day week, where employees earn the same money but work fewer days. This sort of policy may become the norm in a future where work is altogether more human, more creative and more valuable.

As a society, we may even need to re-evaluate what matters to us and the things that we're proud of. As the world of work changes, hopefully we'll come to value and acquire status beyond what we do for a living, how many hours a week we work, or how much money we earn. Could AI help us create a future in which caring for a parent is seen as just as valuable as paid work? I hope so. I hope AI will make us *more* human.

Of course, it could go the other way. AI could serve to widen economic disparity, hasten climate change, plunge sections of society into deeper poverty, and create a gap between the haves and the have-nots that we'll never be able to close. To avoid that, we need to take steps in the right direction now. (As a starting point, I recommend looking at the United Nations Sustainable Development Goals.[8] These goals are designed to address some of the issues already mentioned, including inequality, poverty and climate change, to create a better, more sustainable future.)

In order to build this bright future, where the intelligence revolution positively serves humans and our societies:

- Organizations will need to recognize and value the human contribution, and remember that people will remain the biggest asset a company has.
- Organizations will also need to ensure they use AI in an ethical, responsible and safe way (see Chapter 9). We'll see more regulation to help guide this.
- The technology itself must step up to provide solutions to some of AI's specific problems, such as data security, the black box issue (or lack of explainability), and the threat to individual privacy. New tools like homomorphic encryption (see Chapter 10) will help with this.
- At a societal level, we'll need some serious rethinks around what matters, what we value, and how we reward that value. Redistributing income or creating a universal basic income provide some solutions. (Interestingly, Bill Gates has proposed that robots pay income tax, which could help to pay for reskilling people whose jobs have been displaced by automation.[9])
- And we all need to be asking ourselves, 'What serves us and makes our lives better?' If the use of AI doesn't serve us or make our lives better, we really shouldn't be doing it.

Ultimately, we have an enormous opportunity in front of us: a chance to use the most powerful technology we've ever had to make a real difference. This is our choice, our responsibility, and our privilege.

## Staying in touch

If you would like to continue to learn about the intelligence revolution, or better even, activity participate in the dialogue, then let's connect. I am active on the following platforms, which all offer different ways of sharing content and discussing this exciting topic:

- **LinkedIn:** Bernard Marr
- **Twitter:** @bernardmarr
- **YouTube:** Bernard Marr
- **Instagram:** @bernardmarr
- **Facebook:** facebook.com/BernardWMarr

You can also head for my website at www.bernardmarr.com for more content as well as an opportunity to join my weekly newsletter, in which I share all the very latest information.

I regularly write for *Forbes* and I am always on the lookout for new examples, success stories and topics for my column. Let me know if you have anything you would like me to share or explore. And finally, if you think I could help you or your business with making the most of the intelligence revolution, then get in touch.

## Endnotes

1  Marr, B (2020) *Technology Trends in Practice: How AI, blockchains, augmented reality and other digital innovations are transforming businesses*, John Wiley & Sons

2  Snow, J (2019) How artificial intelligence can tackle climate change, *National Geographic*, https://www.nationalgeographic.co.uk/science-and-technology/2019/07/how-artificial-intelligence-can-tackle-climate-change (archived at https://perma.cc/4S4M-EKAC)

3  Marr, B (2018) How artificial intelligence can help fight world hunger, *SAP insider*, https://sapinsider.wispubs.com/Assets/Articles/2018/January/How-Artificial-Intelligence-Can-Help-Fight-World-Hunger (archived at https://perma.cc/W954-5UKW)

4  Hallotan, T (2017) How Atlassian went from 10% female technical graduates to 57% in two years, *Textio*, https://textio.com/blog/how-atlassian-went-from-10-female-technical-graduates-to-57-in-two-years/13035166507 (archived at https://perma.cc/2ANM-D2NL)

5  Kashyap, S and Gattiker, A (2017) Clarifying the complex with a 'simpler voice', *IBM*, https://www.ibm.com/blogs/think/2017/07/simpler-voice/ (archived at https://perma.cc/7V8G-SLDM)

6  Fake News Challenge, http://www.fakenewschallenge.org/ (archived at https://perma.cc/RW7P-DJ4T)

7  Polakovic, G (2019) The next big effort in AI: keeping LA's water flowing post-earthquake, *USC News*, https://news.usc.edu/160680/ai-la-water-supply-earthquake-usc-research/ (archived at https://perma.cc/69E2-KYYY)

8  Sustainable Development Goals, United Nations, https://www.un.org/sustainabledevelopment/sustainable-development-goals/ (archived at https://perma.cc/4MDN-TEA3)

9  Waters, R (2017) Bill Gates calls for income tax on robots, *Financial Times*, https://www.ft.com/content/d04a89c2-f6c8-11e6-9516-2d969e0d3b65 (archived at https://perma.cc/DE4L-3ZJ4)

# Templates

A key message in this book has been that businesses must approach the intelligence revolution in their own organization strategically. In order to help companies identify the AI use cases and an AI strategy, as outlined in detail in Chapter 7, I have developed two templates. You can download electronic versions of these templates from my website at www.bernardmarr.com.

FIGURE T.1    AI use case template

**1. Link to strategic goal**

**What is the strategic business goal that this AI use case will support?**

**2. Objective**

**What are the objectives of this AI use case?**

**3. Measures of success (KPIs)**

**How will success be measured? What business metrics will this initiative impact? What will be the key results?**

**4. Use case owner**

**Who will be the owner or sponsor of this AI use case?**

**5. AI approach and required data**

**What AI approach are you planning to use and what data will be required?**

**6. Ethical and legal issues**

**Are there any ethical or legal issues regarding this use case? (privacy, GDPR, bias)**

FIGURE T.1   *continued*

7. Technology and
   infrastructure

What are the technology and
infrastructure challenges and
requirements?

8. Skills and capacity

What are the challenges
around skills, capabilities,
capacity and resourcing?

9. Implementation

What are the implementation
challenges? Who will deliver
the project? (in-house,
outsourced, hybrid,
partnerships)

10. Change management

Which employees will be
affected by this project and
how will the change be
managed?

Extra notes

FIGURE T.2  AI strategy template

Major use cases (1–5): Use case 1, Use case 2, Use case 3

Quick wins (1–3): Use case 4, Use case 5

**Strategic use cases** (customer value proposition, new products or services, automate processes)

**Cross-cutting goals**

**Data strategy** — A solid data strategy should underpin an AI strategy

**Ethical and legal** (AI bias, privacy, ethical approach) — eg Cross-cutting ethical and legal issue 1 · eg Cross-cutting ethical and legal issue 2

**Technology and infrastructure** (cloud, distributed computing, data layers) — eg Cross-cutting technology and infrastructure issue 1

**Skills and capacity** (skill gaps, training requirements, in-sourcing, outsourcing, partnering) — eg Cross-cutting skills and capacity issue 1 · eg Cross-cutting skills and capacity issue 2

**Implementation** (skill gaps, training requirements, in-sourcing, outsourcing, partnering) — eg Cross-cutting implementation issue 1

**Change management** (user and employee impact, communication, engagement, change management) — eg Cross-cutting skills change management issue 1 · eg Cross-cutting skills change management issue 2

# INDEX

CPSIA information can be obtained
at www.ICGtesting.com
Printed in the USA
LVHW052130220820
663800LV00006B/18

9 781789 664348